Haiku

Dodoitsu

and

Waka

A Zen Harvest

JAPANESE FOLK ZEN SAYINGS

Compiled and Translated with an Introduction by
SŌIKU SHIGEMATSU

Foreword by
ROBERT AITKEN

NORTH POINT PRESS

Printed in the United States of America
Library of Congress Catalogue Card Number: 87-82594
ISBN: 0-86547-328-5
SECOND PRINTING
Calligraphy courtesy of the translator.

North Point Press

Contents

For Maya and Sōjun

Foreword

There is no concept or archetype in Zen Buddhism that does not self-destruct. The Diamond Sutra says, "The Buddha does not have the thirty-two marks of the Buddha, therefore he (or she) is called Buddha." Buddha, shunyata, prajna, maya—all are provisional.

With such transparent and ephemeral terminology and imagery Zen Buddhism becomes American, Australian, Polish, and Argentine, while Confucianism remains Chinese, however skillfully it is translated. Heidegger remains German in the most fluent Japanese. Zen is poetry, as R. H. Blyth said.[1] Poetry might use unfamiliar words and names, but these can be looked up, and when they are clear East and West can smile together.

> Paradise is
> None of my business, but
> I've got to go
> Help Amitabha Buddha
> Who works there.

I find this Dharma song in Sōiku Shigematsu's collection to be reminiscent of Gary Snyder's American haiku:

> You be Bosatsu,
> I'll be the taxi driver
> Driving you home.[2]

Amitabha is the Buddha of Infinite Light and Life who guides us to the Western Paradise when we die. Bosatsu is Bodhisattva, the enlightened being, the being who is becoming enlightened, and the being who enlightens others. Both poems poke gentle fun at these noble fellows and

[1] R. H. Blyth, *Zen in English Literature and Oriental Classics* (New York: Dutton, 1960), pp. viii, 25 ff.

[2] Gary Snyder, *Earth Household* (New York: New Directions, 1969), p. 10.

present the Buddha's disciple who wears no label at all. The Diamond Sutra outdone!

I look forward to seeing anthologies of Western poetry and folk sayings that are designed to enhance study for Western Zen students. Meanwhile, here is Shigematsu Sensei's splendid English version of poems selected for Japanese Zen students, completely accessible for all of us.

—*Robert Aitken*

Acknowledgments

I would like to offer my deepest gratitude, first of all, to Robert Aitken Rōshi for his foreword to this book. My father happened to be one of his earliest teachers who taught him formal zazen at the Engaku-ji monastery in Kamakura. He then had a chance to visit Shōgen-ji, our temple, in 1950 and I "saw" him for the first time when I was a little boy. The fact is, he and I have known each other for almost forty years.

My sincere thanks goes to Gary Snyder, always my most reliable advisor, who has done a lot of kindnesses to me for the past ten years, including his sponsorship for my stay at the University of California at Davis as a Fulbright scholar in 1987 and his invaluable foreword for *A Zen Forest*, my first Zen saying anthology. Again with regard to the present collection, his generous assistance was great in many ways (and actually two poems translated by him are included here).

I am especially indebted to Professor Dan McLeod of San Diego State University, who, as an almost professional copy editor, checked my second manuscript very carefully, polishing it up into the third and final one. Groping sometimes for the best expressions with a pencil in his hand, Dan often muttered, "Damn! Oh, no! Damn!"

My warm thanks go to Professor Lowell Tozer, who read my manuscript and was a thoughtful and kind neighbor during my stay in San Diego. Especially to Ms. Kyōko Ōta, who made for me pieces of beautiful calligraphy, which adorn this book, and also to North Point people, Jack Shoemaker, Tom Christensen, Kate Moses, and the others, who have made my manuscript into book form. And to all those others who helped and encouraged me at each stage of my efforts.

Lastly, I must mention Maya, my daughter, who was born with foot trouble in 1981 when *A Zen Forest* was published and I started the present work, and whose "thundering" cries often disturbed my concentration. Most of this work, however, was done in the lobby of the Shizuoka Children's Hospital while I waited so many times for her coming out of the examination room with her mother. Maya had to undergo four big operations, but fortunately the whole trouble my family shared has so far disappeared and has turned into this book.

Shōgen-ji Zen temple, Shimizu
January 1988

Introduction

To me Zen is a bit like the *mikan* trees that grow in our temple orchard. The *mikan* is a kind of mandarin orange that we harvest in late autumn. Every year, I make it a rule to take my son, Sōjun, into the orchard to let him learn something of Zen from *mikan*-picking. At this time of the year, all the *mikan* branches are heavy with ripe fruit. Just looking at them makes me restless. I feel as though it were my urgent business to release each tree from its heavy burden. The drooping branch is my drooping heart. It's not good for a burdened heart to bear any more than it has to. And like the bending *mikan* trees, the burden should not be carried indefinitely. Unload and just enjoy the freedom of it.

> How refreshing
> The whinny of a packhorse
> Unloaded of everything! *(327)*

As we set to work, each of us hangs from his shoulder a bamboo basket, into which we place the picked fruit. I say to Sōjun, "Don't toss the fruit in so roughly. Be careful with it or you'll bruise it. It's as alive as we are, so treat it as carefully as you would your own eyeball, as Dōgen Zenji says. Treat it roughly and watch its sweetness go. It'll lose its freshness and rot to spite you.

"And don't seal up that vinyl bag we put fruit in. See how damp the inside of the bag has become. That shows the fruit is breathing even after it's picked from the twig. Leave it open a little so the fruit can breathe. It's really like us that way.

"Do you know why this fruit is so green? It's because it didn't get enough sunshine. And why these pieces are so small? Because this tree's roots couldn't grow deep enough or spread wide enough through the soil. It needs more nourishment. Its puniness is its way of asking for help. Let's listen to its voiceless words. We've got to cultivate the earth more deeply around these trees."

Sometimes when Sōjun thinks he's finished a tree, I say, "You think you're done, but I can see some pieces still left hanging. There! Over there! Yes, that one near the top hidden behind the leaves. It's not easy to see. Another's down there below that branch. You can see it better from this angle. Come over here, you can see it clearly." My talk goes on like this in the *mikan* orchard.

This is the Zen priest in me speaking, suggesting that with a slight shift in the angle of vision, some bit of truth shows itself of its own accord. Sticking to one angle is the worst thing: flexibility is all. Zen, like the *mikan* tree, should be approached from various viewpoints.

In the following, I shall introduce Japanese folk Zen sayings, according to three fundamental angles of vision:

(1) Zen Universalism

(2) Zen Individualism

(3) Zen Vitalism.[1]

To these, I wish to add another important aspect of Zen, which present-day people might call:

(4) Zen Ecology.

But, before we start, let's take a quick look at the historical aspect of the Zen sayings that comprise this anthology.

One of the most vital parts of traditional koan study as practiced in the Rinzai Zen monasteries of Japan has been *jakugo* or capping-phrase exercises.

The first thing every newcomer to the *zendō* (meditation hall) has to do is become used to sitting in concentration without any physical or mental disturbance. Once this is accomplished, the student is given a koan such as the well-known "What is the sound of one hand (clapping)?" by the *rōshi* (Zen master). After this the student devotes all his or her energy to this koan, a question that cannot be dealt with by intellectual analysis. This study often takes a long time, but when at last an appropriate response has been successfully offered and confirmed, the student can move on to the next step in the process—the *jakugo* exercise. That is, the student is required to pick out the most appropriate capping phrase, usually a passage in a poem from among thousands in a special anthology, that best explains the physical-and-mental state the student has reached.

[1]This terminology comes from the three traditional categories of Buddhist philosophy: *tai* (substance), *sō* (characteristic), and *yū* (activity).

In the zendo, no books are allowed except this anthology, a capping-phrase book. Every student is expected to keep at least one copy of such an anthology, usually inside a sleeve of his or her monk's robe to be read through again and again. Zen students find this exercise really useful, even inevitable, because of the help it provides them in clarifying their views of each koan. By practicing this exercise, students naturally learn the handbook sayings by heart, and this constitutes the basic culture of Zen people while it also fosters a penetrating eye for classic Zen texts.

But more important, this exercise is a paradoxical attempt, within a spiritual discipline that normally eschews dependence on language, to express the unexplainable Zen experience poetically. Thus it serves as an invaluable bridge connecting two seemingly incompatible worlds: the world of literature and the unexplainable world of Zen experience.

Compiled in the late fifteenth century by the Japanese Zen master, Tōyō Eichō (1428–1504), the *Zenrin Kushū* (Zen Forest Saying Anthology) is the time-honored capping-phrase book.[2] This collection of Zen phrases and sayings was plucked from a variety of Chinese sources, not all of which are specifically Buddhist. Besides such Zen classics as *The Blue Cliff Records* and *The Gateless Gate*, Tōyō drew from the Confucian *Analects*, T'ang and Sung poetry, and many other Chinese sources. So far as traditional koan study is concerned, the *Zenrin Kushū*, the essence of Zen literature, serves the student as an authentic map of the main road to Zen.

Another handbook, the *Zenrin Segoshū* (Folk Zen Saying Anthology) was compiled to meet the demands of those who find the *Zenrin Kushū* difficult to read because its entries are written entirely in Chinese.[3]

Since Chinese characters were introduced to Japan as early as the fourth century, the Japanese share a vast written vocabulary with the Chinese people. For the Japanese to absorb these Chinese ideographs it

[2]My English translation of more than 1,200 Zen sayings from capping-phrase books is now available. Sōiku Shigematsu: *A Zen Forest: Sayings of the Masters* (New York & Tokyo: Weatherhill, 1981). Gary Snyder's foreword places this collection in its historical background and in wider contemporary perspectives.

[3]Three different collections have appeared in book form: the most recent edition is the one by Etsudō Tsuchiya, *Zenrin Segoshū* (Kyoto: Kichudō, 1957). Mostly from these collections, I have picked out what seem to me the most relevant to the present anthology, which is a companion to my earlier *A Zen Forest*. I have taken care, therefore, in my translations to emphasize as much as possible the Zen implications of each poem. *Tanka* is translated into five lines; *dodoitsu*, four; *haiku*, three. All the entries in this book are arranged in the Japanese alphabetical (*a-i-u-e-o*) order of the original Japanese poems.

was, of course, necessary to fit them into the context of their own language. The principal adjustment was one of word order. Thus, despite the similar appearance of the two written languages, they are fundamentally different.

Quite naturally, as Zen became popular among laymen who knew only Japanese, the Japanese Zen masters and priests had to create a new literary tradition. Although they continued to write poems and sermons in classical Chinese, the traditional written language of Japanese Zen Buddhism, the practice of writing the words of the Dharma in their native language gradually became increasingly common among Zen teachers in Japan. Those who were good poets have not only extended the Buddhist world but have simultaneously enriched the body of Japanese literature.

The *Zenrin Segoshū* is thus a collection of Japanese *tanka* (*waka*), *haiku* (*hokku*), and other short traditional Japanese literary forms suitable for practicing the capping-phrase exercise. Some entries are the *waka* of famous Japanese Zen masters such as Dōgen (1200–53), Ikkyū (1394–1481), Bunan (1603–76), Hakuin (1685–1768), and Ryōkan (1757–1831). Others are by lay students such as Miyamoto Musashi (?–1645), the famous swordsman and author of *The Book of Five Rings*, or Ninomiya Sontoku (1787–1856), a well-known intellectual and leader of an agricultural movement. And a number of the *haiku* are by Japan's greatest poets: Bashō (1644–94), Buson (1718–83), Issa (1763–1827), as well as lesser known authors.

The *dodoitsu*, another major Japanese poetic form (though little known abroad), is also represented in this anthology. It is a sort of popular song that originated in the entertainment quarters of nineteenth-century Japan. The themes of these songs are generally amorous and the composers wrote them with no Zen intention at all. But, quite curiously, many of them suggest a good deal about Zen, and that is why so many *dodoitsu* were selected to illustrate Zen points of view.

While it is true that the didactic poems by Zen masters are impressive and have contributed to the illumination of many Zen students, some readers may find the real gems of the collection to be the secular sayings by ordinary people, who devoted their brief lives to the transient whims of this ephemeral world. Behind their laughter and complaints, we can hear their authentic human voices. The *Zenrin Segoshū* is, so to speak, a storehouse of poems of enlightenment through unenlightenment.

I. ZEN UNIVERSALISM

Shakyamuni abandoned his wife, son, and the Capila Castle at the age of twenty-nine. He could have enjoyed his happy, secular life as a prince of the Shakya clan, were it not for the doubts that grew gradually and secretly in the depth of his heart. One day, the story goes, he was out in his chariot when he happened to meet successively an old man, a sick man, and a corpse. Seeing in them the human sufferings of old age, sickness, and death, Shakyamuni came to realize fully the inevitable facts and uncertainties of life. Every existence, once it comes into being, changes and dies. Nothing in the world remains constant. What Shakyamuni sought was the unchangeable truth behind these ephemeral phenomena. So, cutting all secular bonds, he left home. This is the story of his "great renunciation."

To recognize the impermanence of existence is the beginning of self-realization.

Young and old—
Whoever they are—
Their bodies are
More fragile than the dew
On the morning glory. *(105)*

Now, now,
This now is
A time for good-bye;
Disappearing like the dew
My life, your life. *(67)*

Human life, as the Japanese commonplace expresses it, is as fleeting as dew. It disappears in the twinkling of an eye. This bitterest of truths to which we must resign ourselves is the major theme of the *Zenrin Segoshū*.

Life is transient. It has no entity. Every existence is merely a temporary compound of elements.

Where and what is
"I"?
It's only
A temporary ball of
Earth-water-fire-wind. *(50)*

These four elements just happened to gather themselves into that karmic "ball," which constitutes our "self." When they come apart, we must depart—into the original Void.

> Pull and bind the sheaves
> Of grass together:
> There's a grass hut.
> Untie them and, there,
> The original field. *(535)*

Behind all illusory phenomena, the original Nothing prevails.

> When the lantern goes out,
> Where, I wonder, does
> Its light go?
> Darkness is my own
> Original house. *(408)*

"Hello, darkness my old friend / I've come to talk with you again," goes Paul Simon's song, "The Sound of Silence." "Country roads, take me home to the place I belong," sings John Denver. These two American popular singers recall, in their own kind of "waka," the place where we finally return. All individual lives—grass, fish, dog, mankind—dissolve and vanish soon enough into the Darkness. Yes, we return home to the void, the universe, the whole. It is Nothing, our original home, from which we have come.

To reach it is the way to Nirvana. By denying our "self" we become Nothing, and cosmic consciousness arises.

> What is
> Mind like,
> I wonder.
> Its invisible, and
> As large as the universe. *(262)*

Now, we are the universe itself.

> A hand-rolled
> Dumpling of
> Heaven-and-earth:
> I've gulped it down
> And easily it went. *(397)*

I've thrust away
The man who gulped the dumpling
Of heaven-and-earth
With the
Tip of my eyelash. *(398)*

This cosmic consciousness provokes a kind of optimism, in which every distinction is blotted out. Individuality is meaningless. Seeing all in oneness is our goal here.

Life and death in
This passing world—
See through them
And they're like
Ice and water. *(39)*

It makes no more sense grieving over death than it does birth because they are one thing from the viewpoint of this Universalism. Fortune and misfortune are one and the same. Gain and loss, good and bad, love and hatred, young and old, rich and poor—all are one. Absolute Oneness dominates this world.

Rain, hail,
Snow, ice:
All different, but
They finally meld into
One valley stream. *(19)*

Viewed from this universal perspective, man is a mere "temporary ball," a speck of dust in this boundless cosmos. Life disappears so quickly that any sense of "self" is mere deception.

Loved wife, hated husband
In the end,
Under a mossy tomb,
Both skulls. *(324)*

How odd T. S. Eliot's Prufrock is! "Do I dare?" "Do I dare?"[4] Why hesitate? What is the self you cling to so anxiously, Prufrock?

[4]"The Love Song of J. Alfred Prufrock" in *Collected Poems: 1909–1962* (London: Faber, 1963).

Just put off
Attachment
From your mind:
This world is
Paradise. *(117)*

Zen reveals itself in subtle ways when our nihilism reaches its darkest depths.

2. ZEN INDIVIDUALISM

Returning from the Original Nothing—the world of no entity, no individuality—here we must meet a second aspect of Zen.

The One Mind
Of heaven and earth
Is dyed into
A thousand different
Grass colors. *(23)*

This is it. The "One Mind" reveals itself in "a thousand different grass colors." Out of it come respectively animals, fish, worms, trees, rocks—and human beings, too. Here, individuality counts for something and difference is admired.

Of course, some are wise and some are otherwise. Everything enjoys its own originality. In this way each phenomenon becomes a koan.

In spring, flowers;
Summer, cuckoos;
Autumn, moon.
In winter, snow is
Chilling and cool. *(528)*

With such diversity, everything becomes our teacher. So long as we are selfless, each being reveals its own secret to us. In this sense Zen students are like ecologists whose understanding of organisms is through their interrelationships with others.

Each existence in this world is the one-and-only piece of work by the "One Mind," that is, the whole universe.

All heaven and earth
Have worked out

This single buttercup:
Surely it will go on
Age after age. *(24)*

One buttercup opens as a result of an infinite accumulation of causes and effects from time immemorial.

That the whole universe is a void is not to deny it is also an apparatus of the highest intricacy and sophistication. Everything is most elaborately created through incredibly complex networks of interdependence such as the food chains.

Horse dung originates in
The pampas grass—on
The hills and fields—which
Once gave shelter to
Chirping grasshoppers. *(90)*

In perfect ecological harmony, each being shining bright because everything is unique.

Winds play the *shamisen*,
Leaves flutter and dance,
Dawn crows
Start singing. *(165)*

Winds, leaves, crows—each one is doing its own original job, and all are in perfect harmony at the same time.

This is the view of Zen Individualism. It is individualism supported by Zen Universalism. Needless to say, it is quite different from egotism or isolationism.

My body is given up,
Cast away,
Zero.
But on snowy nights
I feel chilly. *(86)*

Having abandoned myself, I am Nothing and have no senses. Nevertheless, I'm cold on snowy nights. Why?

I know well enough these
Cherry blossoms will

> Return to dust, but I
> Find it hard to leave
> The trees in full bloom. *(482)*

Though I understand that every existence is without entity, from the bottom of my heart, I love and cling to these cherry flowers in full bloom. Why?

We go on denying our "self"—making ourselves into Nothing: this is Zen Universalism. From there we have returned with a particular kind of self-affirmation that sees everything with innocent eyes again. John Steinbeck, no more consciously a Buddhist than the anonymous composers of *dodoitsu*, put it this way:

> It is advisable to look
> From the tide pool
> To the stars and then
> Back to the tide pool again.[5]

"Back to the tide pool again." Yes! This tide pool, here and now, is where Zen people live, treasuring each and every moment as a priceless jewel.

> Never, never
> Neglect your life though it's
> Temporary:
> Your present life, fleeting,
> Is the only one that's yours. *(184)*

This is Zen Individualism.

3. ZEN VITALISM

In Zen, vitality is highly admired.

> Walking is Zen:
> sitting, too.[6]

Zazen is not everything. Releasing the inner vitality each being possesses originally is the vitalism of Zen.

> Be thoroughly,
> Dead

[5] *The Log from the Sea of Cortez* (New York: Viking, 1951), p. 217. Line breaks are mine.
[6] Sōiku Shigematsu, *A Zen Forest* (New York and Tokyo: Weatherhill, 1981), poem no. 253.

While alive!
Do just as you wish:
All you do is best. *(40)*

This saying does not recommend suicide. Every Zen student must free himself from his superficial self. We must extinguish it completely if we are to follow our original Self and so live consentaneously with truth.

Universalism is expressed in the first and second lines, and Individualism in the third and fourth: both are animated into Vitalism in the fourth and fifth. These three aspects, seen from three different angles of vision, eventually resolve into a single, original truth: Zen Universal-Individual-Vitalism.

Zen is neither a bystander's philosophy nor a principle, but an all-embracing human activity, a way of life, a way of identification—a subtle way of establishing our own subjecthood in no-mindedness. It is also an art of transcending dualism.

The bell ringing?
Or is it the stick ringing?
Between the bell and the stick,
It rings. *(174)*

It is the origin of All. Penetrate it!

The fruit as it hangs
Becomes a sweet cake:
Persimmon. *(311)*

A persimmon's bitter fruit turns first from green to yellow and the greatest change—the point here—is that its bitterness changes to sweetness although it simply remains hanging on the twig, and there seems no change between before and after. In this way, the saying suggests, worldly passion turns naturally into satori, since both are originally one and inseparable from each other.[7] From this unity comes Zen activity beyond yes and no, good and bad.

Zen gives a hint to a problem of subjectivity.

Both heaven and hell
Are inside

[7]See *A Zen Forest*, no. 1096.

> Yourself;
> Devils or Buddhas are
> Nothing but your heart. *(254)*

Everything is up to our no-minded self.

> The ship depends on sail,
> The sail depends on wind;
> I, a merchant,
> Depend on the customers. *(558)*

Willows are another good example of no-minded subjectivity.

> Depending on the wind:
> Twining or untwining . . .
> Meek-minded
> Weeping willows. *(649)*

One of the most precious lessons Dōgen Zenji learned during his stay in China was the importance of this flexibility of mind. No-minded like a drifting cloud, like flowing water: this is the Zen way, the core of the Zen spirit. Cast off that human bondage you carry on your shoulder. Unload and abandon it at once. No-minded flexibility really helps here.

The Japanese people use, unfortunately less frequently now, the *furoshiki*, a thin cloth of cotton or silk for wrapping and carrying things. It may serve as a symbol of Zen Vitalism. In this square piece of cloth, we can pack up almost anything because the cloth changes, faithfully following the shape of the article it wraps. It's in marked contrast to the inflexibility of a hard, stiff suitcase. When not in use, the *furoshiki* can be folded and refolded like a handkerchief that's easily kept in our pockets. When we find ourselves without one, we can use the *furoshiki* as a substitute. When rain comes, it turns into a shelter. Since it's often beautifully dyed and patterned, sometimes it serves as a scarf. And its last service may be as a floorcloth.

Love, too, explains Zen Vitalism.

> Whatever happens to me
> Concerns me not at all.
> I could throw my life away
> For your sake! *(363)*

The devotion to oneness in this poem is samadhi; its concentration on "you" is "love samadhi." Very good! Samadhi is a fundamental element that pervades Zen.

On my way to you
A thousand miles become one:
Across the wide rice field,
Just a jump— *(584)*

Such single-minded concentration can produce miracles. Sometimes it transforms impossibility into possibility.

It is a great pity we are surrounded with so many things that distract and dissipate our attention. In the face of avarice which appears boundless, Zen recommends "plain living and high thinking." To put ourselves in samadhi, it urges with Thoreau that we simplify our lives. While eating, we should maintain eating-samadhi, by not doing something else, such as watching television at the same time. Reading a newspaper will dispel shitting-samadhi. Eating and shitting are the sacred ceremonies of reception and repayment, and thanksgiving to Nature; don't they deserve our single-minded respect? Become food! Turn into shit!

4. ZEN ECOLOGY

Zen followers have always embraced the ecological point of view. They see all in each and each in all, macrocosm in microcosm and microcosm in macrocosm: all nature in one great harmony. They live in the love of nature, and always see themselves as a part of all—despite the humbling awareness that as human beings we are newcomers to the history of life (3,000,000,000 years old) on this earth (4,500,000,000 years old) in this universe (12,000,000,000 years old). Compare the history of the earth to a calendar year: ego-centered modern man showed up only a few seconds before the very end of the last day of the year, December 31. We may boast of our intellect, or bask in our position as the most highly evolved of creatures at the top of a food chain, but the fact remains we are no other than the latest comers to the animal kingdom. Since we owe them our lives, we should revere our predecessors on this earth.

A heavy snowfall . . .
Disappears into the sea.
What silence! *(110)*

Here's the sea, the origin of all life. Aeons ago, mother-sea gave birth to the first bit of life. Through cell division tiny lives appeared, and in the long process of evolution, fish, amphibians, reptiles, birds, and then mammals inhabited this earth. That unborn babies repeat in condensed form this overwhelmingly long history of life while in their mothers' womb is a wonderfully appropriate way to begin a human life. Amniotic fluid, it is said, is constituted in almost the same way as sea water. Bathing in this ancient mother-sea, the embryo shows a fish's fin, sprouts a lizard's tail, and a waterfowl's web joins its fingers and toes. Truly, every existence is a microcosm, and all creatures are our relatives from the one original life. We can't live without the other members of the earth, of the universe. We are one family interdependent upon each other.

Sometimes, however, we human beings are a drag on that family, a burden to the ecosystem. Some people hunt and kill their brothers and sisters for only fun or money. Some destroy mountains and forests, pollute rivers and seas, while others try to keep air and water and earth clean. Launchers of artificial satellites scatter their dust in space, polluting that stardust which is our own garden.

My hut's roof is
The blue heavens;
Floor, the earth;
Lamps, the sun and moon;
Hand-broom, the wind. *(746)*

We must keep our "Universe-House-Hold" (a coinage from Gary Snyder's *Earth House Hold*) just as it goes because the universe is our dearest home. Loving nature is simply loving ourselves. Injuring it is injuring ourselves.

Don't pick it up,
Just leave it there:
A clover in the field. *(393)*

Showing perfection, a clover shines all around when it stands as it is in the field.

Everyone wants
To break off a branch, but they
Look better at a distance:
Cherry flowers in full bloom. *(126)*

The full-blooming cherry flowers are most beautiful viewed in harmony with the whole of surrounding nature.

> Hey, don't hit him!
> The fly rubs his hands,
> Rubs his legs. *(692)*

Ahimsa (don't injure!) is the first precept of all Buddhists. We are not to needlessly kill or injure anything. We must admit in reverence the fact that every creature has received its own irreplaceable life.

Santiago, the old fisherman in Hemingway's *The Old Man and the Sea*, hooking one of a pair of marlin, "begged her pardon and butchered her promptly."[8] Yes, Santiago is exactly right. He is a Zen fisherman. All we can do is apologize to the fish we are going to eat—because life lives on other lives. What an irony! When, driven by necessity, we kill other creatures, we should feel the pain of compassion for whatever life we have taken—whales, dolphins, beef cattle—along with profound gratitude for their manifold sacrifices that have made our lives possible.

We have a Buddhist ceremony of freeing birds and fish from captivity. A Release Pond is often dug in the precincts of a Buddhist temple for releasing caught fish.

> The tadpoles: at once
> All eaten by the fish that's
> Released to the Release Pond.

But here, ironically enough, it is the fish that has been waiting—with its mouth wide open—for the released tadpoles. It is the nature of creatures that all are arranged in the food chain. Thus a Buddhist makes *gasshō* as a token of apology and gratitude, joining his or her hands together at the palms and raising them to the breast.

> The two palms in *gasshō*:
> Right, the enlightened;
> Left, the unenlightened.
> Between them,
> One cry of Buddha. *(612)*

Or, as a Zen-ecologist with absolute love of nature has said:

[8] *The Old Man and the Sea* (New York: Scribners, 1952), p. 50.

When I die,
Don't burn the corpse,
Don't bury it;
Just throw it in a field,
Feed a hungry dog! *(769)*

Buddhists perform memorial services even for lifeless things, not simply the deceased. *Hari-kuyō*, held on February 8 every year, is an example of this practice. It is a requiem service, for the broken needles we have used, to express our gratitude to them. The participants in turn put useless needles into a piece of *tōfu* or soybean curd, making *gasshō*.

In chanting-samadhi,
No myself,
No Buddha:
"Namu Amida-butsu!"
"Namu Amida-butsu!" *(405)*

This is how the Great Mind that is ours works—shedding its own original radiance. Right there: Zen Universal-Individual-Vitalism.

JAPANESE FOLK ZEN SAYINGS

1 Each time wishing
Beforehand to talk it out,
I've never parted from you
Without feeling many words
Unspoken . . .

2 The pepper husk is
Still green, but watch out!
It's hot.

3 Autumn coming—
It's almost unnoticed, but
I feel its
Invisible arrival
In the rustling winds.

4 Autumn now!
Some clouds chasing the moon,
Others running away.

5 The moon on
Each drop of
Dew on each blade of
Each grass stalk in
The autumn field.

As if carrying in my hand 6
The whole field of autumn:
An insect-box.

Your job itself 7
Is "the sound of
One hand clapping";
No use using
Both hands.

Had you done a good job 8
Clapping with
Two hands,
No need then to hear
The sound of one.

Given it up, you say? 9
But what have you given up?
Very well, you've given up
The idea of giving up.

The morning glory 10
Seems transient enough, but
More transient is the
Dew that falls from its petal,
Shattered and scattered.

11 From morning till night
You see it, but if
Absent-minded, everything is
Nothing but farting or wind.

12 Morning's sleepy-head,
Afternoon napping,
Early bedtime:
What? He's awake! Oh,
Dozing . . .

13 It seems useless, but
Don't throw it away;
Sour young grapes
Finally grow into
Sweet raisins.

14 A snake without feet
Crawls;
A fish without ears
Listens to the chirp of a
Cicada without a mouth.

15 Hot and humid night!
Groping for the fan
Half asleep.

Are there? Or not? 16
How interesting—
Snail's horns.

Tomorrow is another day, so 17
I'll take a nap today.
Trotting dogs
Find a bone somewhere.

Making that mountain 18
His own pendant:
Rice planting.

Rain, hail, 19
Snow, ice:
All different, but
They finally meld into
One valley stream.

It's not fine 20
When it's raining.
Elder brother is
Older than I.

21 It began to shower, besides
My sandals are broken;
The dog chases me barking,
But, my door's locked!

22 Rain pouring down,
Dried food getting soaked,
Rice smells burnt,
Baby crying for its milk.

23 The One Mind
Of heaven and earth
Is dyed into
A thousand different
Grass colors.

24 All heaven and earth
Have worked out
This single buttercup:
Surely it will go on
Age after age.

25 Heaven and earth:
Unheard sutra chanting
Repeated . . .

How nice it is! 26
This open sky is
My own house;
I sleep alone in
Mount Sumeru's arms.

The moon 27
Shattered on the shore
Restored to wholeness
In the white water
Receding from the rocks.

No hell exists 28
For those who believe
There's hell, but it
Does for those who
Think there isn't.

There seems, 29
But there's never:
Moon in the water.

Hiding its horns, 30
How round it is:
A snail.

31 "There is," someone says,
And we stick to that "there is."
See there's nothing—
Only the sound
Of the pine wind from the beach.

32 Some say things exist,
Others say not.
Which view is true?
It's like the difference in
Names—water or ice.

33 Zen monk's way goes on
Barrier after barrier,
Like the fifty-three
Stations on the old highway:
As many as horses' farts.

34 Although I came this way
To beg food,
I've spent the time
Picking
Violets in the spring field.

35 No matter
Who he is,
Holy or not,
Make his words your own
If they're true.

I shouldn't mention it. 36
Nevertheless—
Today's heat!

Living in a rented house, 37
No family, no friends:
"Help! Almighty
Bacchus Buddha!"

Talking about it 38
Makes me gloomy;
Not talking, irritated.
Before yes-no thinking is
The world of Buddha.

Life and death in 39
This passing world—
See through them
And they're like
Ice and water.

Be thoroughly 40
Dead
While alive!
Do just as you wish:
All you do is best.

41 How many times
Have I changed my
Firmly determined mind!
Mind, mind,
How unreliable!

42 I'm resolved to be
Reborn to this world
Again and again
So long as I meet
People who stray.

43 The moon on the pond:
Why is it dirty tonight?
It's the water that's muddy,
Not the bright moon.

44 Over the pond
Every night the moon
Casts its light.
But the water won't be soiled;
The moon won't either.

45 Night after night
The moon shines
On the pond, leaving
No light,
No trace.

The pond is like 46
The human mind:
Sometimes dirty,
Sometimes serene,
Only heaven knows.

The quarrel is 47
Just an
Echo:
Your rival is aggressive
Because you are.

Floating clouds, 48
Sticking
Nowhere,
May fly over
Any mountaintop.

"From where to where 49
Are you going?" you ask.
My answer is:
"From back to forward—
Only my feet know."

Where and what is 50
"I"?
It's only
A temporary ball of
Earth-water-fire-wind.

51 I wish I could grasp
That stone
A thousand feet down
On bottom of the Ise Sea
Without wetting my sleeves!

52 The clear water
Of the Sea of Ise,
Let it be!
I'll live in
This muddy water.

53 Had he not rushed, he
Wouldn't have been drenched!
The sky cleared up soon
After he ran into the rain:
Traveler through the village.

54 Hurry up, all of you, before
The Dharma ferryboat leaves!
Should you miss it,
Who on earth will help you
Reach the other bank?

55 Does the moon
Slip by
With no intention?
It's a messenger warning
That your life is passing.

Where is 56
Buddha,
You ask?
He is somewhere
Around your heart.

Seems always 57
At leisure:
Navel in my belly.

Everyone wishes it would 58
Always stay on the peak:
The cloud like flowers.

Even a mirror that's 59
Not supposed
To lie,
Reflects things in reverse
Right and left.

The serene mind 60
Like the thread untied
From the tangled lump:
I see it in the moon.

61 Lightning strikes
Mixing up
The dark night.

62 A flash of lightning—
Our life is
Gone in a blink.

63 Thunder has shot
The dogs' quarrel
Shattering them both
In a blink.

64 Nothing seems
So transient as
Human life:
The dew on the petal
Of the morning glory.

65 The prayed-for rain
Fell on those who
Didn't want it.

Waiting, waiting, 66
Waiting for his coming—
To my wakeful ears:
The cry of the dawn bird.

Now, now, 67
This now is
A time for good-bye;
Disappearing like the dew
My life, your life.

Had I been from the start 68
What I am now,
I wouldn't
Suffer as I do.

Death so far 69
Has been
None of my business.
Must I also die?
Oh, help! Help!

Should the moon 70
Distinguish
Rich and poor,
It would never brighten
A poor man's hut.

71 Don't say no, my love!
Come closer to me.
You know you're lying on
The edge of our bed.

72 White face, yellow face,
Ugly or beautiful: it's
Hard to change.
But our mind can be changed,
So set it right.

73 Abandon your
Illusory mind
And meditate:
Who is seeing?
Who is listening?

74 By their colors
Flowers attract us, but
Soon they fade, fall, and
Finally turn into dust.

75 His form is unseen,
His voice unheard.
Who is he?
Pine winds on the hill,
Running water in the valley.

Each has 76
His own
Figure and feature;
What they have in common is
That all stick to their lives.

Ask the way 77
Straight to Nirvana
While you're healthy:
Before you set out on a journey
To the other world.

Existence means, 78
People misunderstand,
That there it is;
An echo may answer but
Nothing is there.

How irritating! 79
The features of the frog
Lolling on the water.

Only if you plant them 80
Can you enjoy
The flowers' full bloom.

81 Fish live in streams,
Birds nest in trees;
Human beings dwell
In warm hearts.

82 Duckweed: today
In bloom by the
Other bank of the pond.

83 A nightingale's song,
Voice of the Dharma before
Shakyamuni was born.

84 What power!
A rope has moved
The ox's horn.

85 Saying, "The value of
Honesty is
Known by the lie,"
You lie.

My body is given up, *86*
Cast away,
Zero.
But on snowy nights
I feel chilly.

Beater and beaten *87*
Both know
That everything's
Like dew,
Like lightning.

Bending its head *88*
Is its original nature:
A lily.

The moon never intended *89*
To reflect on the water;
The water never asked
To mirror the moon:
Sarusawa Pond.

Horse dung originates in *90*
The pampas grass—on
The hills and fields—which
Once gave shelter to
Chirping grasshoppers.

91 To be born
And be unborn is one thing:
Penetrate this fact.
Death is
Illusion.

92 A newborn baby,
By and by, grows
Cunning and shrewd:
Farther, farther from Buddha.
What a pity!

93 We're all born
And then
We die:
Shakyamuni, Bodhidharma,
Everyone and all.

94 Yes or no,
Good or bad, all
Arguments are gone:
More beautiful tunes come
From pine winds on the hills.

95 Plum meets nightingale,
Bamboo welcomes sparrow;
But why—do I
Pine only for you!

Layers of snow 96
On the plum branches:
I mistook them for
The eightfold
Petals of the flowers.

Plum flower's fragrance: 97
Pop, out comes the sun—
The mountain path.

The scent of plum blossoms 98
Makes us peek into
Even a beggar's hut.

The plum tree is 99
Plum to its roots,
Seeds and twigs,
Leaves and flowers and fruits,
Everything . . . plum.

Showing its face, then 100
Turning over: a falling
Autumn maple leaf.

23

100

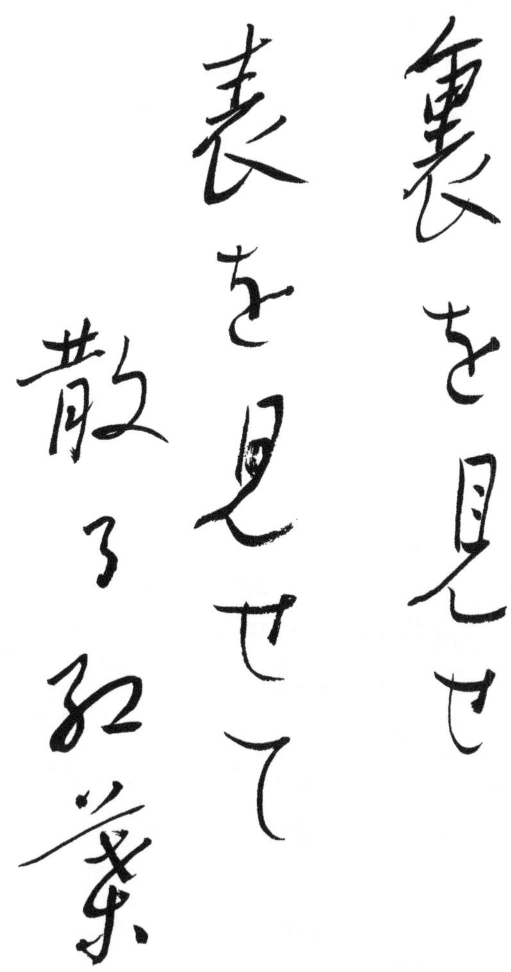

Life is one rest 101
On the way back from Illusion
To Nirvana;
Let it rain if it rains!
Let winds blow if they blow!

The Buddhas: 102
We've drawn pictures,
Carved wooden statues,
But they live
In our hearts.

You're gone, but I'm 103
Still attached to you;
Grasses burn, but their
Roots remain.

Likely to shoot fire 104
Back at the scorching sun:
A gargoyled roof-tile.

Young and old— 105
Whoever they are—
Their bodies are
More fragile than the dew
On the morning glory.

106 How joyous to meet with you!
How terrible to part!
Greeting is the
Beginning of farewell.

107 My wholehearted
Devotion to
You
Made me forget
All about myself.

108 A long drought:
Not even a drop of water
To quarrel over.

109 New Year's Eve,
One fixed day in
A world of change.

110 A heavy snowfall . . .
Disappears into the sea.
What silence!

A clear stream follows 111
Its own way without
Growing into a river.

Ask the sea gulls offshore 112
The time of the tide.
"We're leaving," they'll answer,
"So, ask the waves!"

I really love 113
My barrel-making job;
Connecting each board into
One round barrel.

Walk on deliberately 114
And you'll surely see the world
Beyond the thousand miles,
Even if you walk
As slow as a cow.

Neglect or 115
Effort in summer is
Shown on
The heads of rice
In autumn fields.

116 Don't be too proud!
The round moon is only
One night's life.

117 Just put off
Attachment
From your mind:
This world is
Paradise.

118 Attachment, desire,
Giving them up:
You'll find the world is
All yours.

119 No one is taught
How to fall in love,
But everyone
Learns how
Naturally.

120 How regrettable!
Never
To return:
Days and months, flowing water,
And human lives!

How awesome that 121
Tip of your tongue is!
More terrible than a spearhead
Stabbing,
Destroying you in the end.

How awful! 122
That fire of desire burning,
Burning and burning
Your body, your house
And your friends and all.

Negligence, 123
The dreadful enemy,
Arises . . . just as we
Make our last step after
Ninety-nine steps.

The dreadful edge 124
Of the ice cube is
Originally water.

Quite ready to fall 125
Today—but unnoticed—
Forced to, now, and scattered:
Flowers in the rain.

126 Everyone wants
To break off a branch, but they
Look better at a distance:
  Cherry flowers in full bloom.

127 Man among men:
Otherwise,
No fair lady will
  Fall in love with you!

128 While living in
The same stream,
Herons sleep,
  Cormorants hunt for fish.

129 Why don't you stop
Worrying for good?
Leave it all
  Up to Amitabha Buddha?

130   Mistaken if you
Think you see the moon
  With your own eyes:
You see it with
The light it sheds.

Wisdom, if you 131
Devise it, is
False;
The true wisdom is
What you never know.

I've opened my heart without 132
Undoing my clothes;
I wish you'd notice my feeling
From the cast of my eyes!

Hey, Miss Mount Fuji, 133
Why don't you take off those
Robes of mist?
Wish I could see
Your snow-white skin!

My hair curled elaborately 134
Only for your sake;
It's you who will
Disturb it at midnight.

Up to you: which way 135
This razor goes—
To my eyebrows
Or to my throat?

133

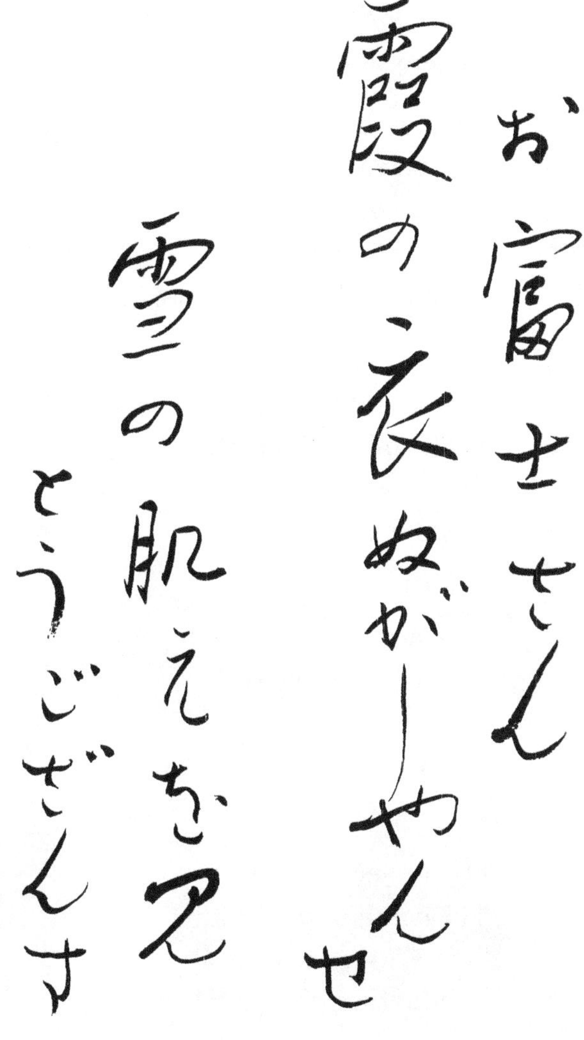

You, till a hundred, 136
I, till ninety-nine:
Both until our hair turns
Gray and white.

Are you awake now? 137
Look here, my dear!
I've got something
To talk about with you.

The world is 138
Like a mirror, you see?
Smile, and your friends
Smile back.

The sharpest cry— 139
Then completely still
Under the flowers:
A bush warbler.

Dare enter into 140
The depth of your heart.
"Here," says a voice:
Who says it? And where?

141 Memories of him:
Tears dropping . . .
Talking of him, wringing
And wringing her sleeve.

142 Remembering him, you say? Then,
You're not really in love.
No remembering, no forgetting:
The secret of true love.

143 No hesitation anymore!
Having already given it all up,
I'm quite ready
To die . . .

144 One desire is
Now achieved;
Then arises the
Next, next, and next . . .
Next to impossible to count.

145 Nothing is
Especially interesting
In this world;
It's our mind that makes it
A really interesting place.

Splendid! 146
Falling autumn leaves,
Flowers in bloom,
Each the exact
Appearance of Dharma.

Used to hang around 147
Women on the streets;
Now churning within him
The flaming wheel of karma.

Why does it mystify itself? 148
That cuckoo:
Only making cries,
Never showing up.

No parents, no friends, 149
No children, no wife,
How lonely!
I would rather
Die!

No parents, 150
No wife,
No children,
No job, no money;
But, no death, thank you.

151 The world is my own!
Even these grasses, for me,
Turn into rice cakes.

152 Pieces of wood,
Broken and burning,
Show different forms,
But their smoke is
The same color.

153 Women's zeal
Pierces the rock;
Even the gold chain can be cut
If you try in earnest.

154 Women,
The storehouse
Of Dharma,
Easily bring forth
Shakyamuni and Bodhidharma.

155 No drop of blood
For you, mosquito, from
My mosquito-like body.

A woman dressed up 156
Over her skeleton:
You call her
An elegant lady?
How funny!

Each enjoys flower-viewing, 157
Dressing up
His own skeleton.

Up to the puppeteer: 158
Out of the doll box
Hung from his neck
Comes a Buddha?
Or a devil?

Wash away everything 159
And winds are cool
On your way back.

Without fences, 160
Everything belongs to me:
The snow-clad mountains.

161 The heat's shimmer
Disappears
Before evening;
Human life is
More fleeting.

162 Not past, not future,
But here and now;
Better than discussion,
Sing, sing.

163 A palanquin bearer
And its passenger,
Both on the same way;
Step by step, nearer
To the destination.

164 If everyone with a similar hat
Were Seijūrō,
Each pilgrimage to Ise Shrine
Would be Seijūrō.

165 Winds play the *shamisen*,
Leaves flutter and dance,
Dawn crows
Start singing.

Wind is your breath; 166
The open sky, your mind;
The sun, your eye;
Seas and mountains,
Your whole body.

Tight buds they seemed, but 167
The spring winds have
Loosened them
Unnoticed.

Looks hard and tight, 168
Soon enough it melts
And flows away:
A snowman.

What shall I leave as 169
A keepsake after I die?
In spring, flowers;
Summer, cuckoos;
Fall, red maple leaves.

A sharp angle creates 170
Bitter feelings;
Mind, mind,
I'll remind you
Just to roll over . . .

171 New Year's pine decoration,
A milestone in our journey
To the other world;
In a sense, it's auspicious,
In another, it's not.

172 All the family
In harmony
Laughing and laughing . . .
This is the original
Music of Nature.

173 A harmonious
Family is
A treasure ship;
It crosses quite smoothly
The ocean of life.

174 The bell ringing?
Or is it the stick ringing?
Between the bell and the stick,
It rings.

175 The bell doesn't ring,
Nor does the stick;
The "between"
Is ringing.

Bell's ringing, 176
Stick's ringing,
The bell-and-stick
Is ringing.

No more money, 177
No more fame;
I need, instead, the one
Penetrating eye!

God, 178
Buddha,
Both are nothing but
The minds of ordinary people,
What else?

When woman combs her hair, 179
Her eyes are
Set.

Since legendary times, 180
Nothing has changed:
Running water and the love
Between woman and man.

181 The lone pine of Karasaki
Has become
Two:
Its shadow cast
On incoming surf.

182 Giving my temporary life
Back to the original
Master,
I only wish happiness to
All people.

183 It's crazy,
In this passing world,
For a lender to feel
He has lent or a borrower
To feel he has borrowed.

184 Never, never
Neglect your life though it's
Temporary:
Your present life, fleeting,
Is the only one that's yours.

185 No bird twitters
On the hillside rice field
After harvest;
Just a scarecrow
Fallen.

Wish I could've taken 186
A picture of you borrowing
Money from me! Wish I'd
Show it to you when you're
Unwilling to repay it!

Don't distinguish 187
Between this and that:
Even a snowman was only
Water, originally.

Crows sitting on 188
A dry branch—
Autumn evening.

Woman and man: 189
They look different
But inside
Their skeletons are
Almost the same.

Were our skins peeled off, 190
Yours and mine,
Which is you?
Which is I?

191 Cold moon:
Sounds of the bridge
As I walk alone.

192 Hysterics:
The next business is
To put things back.

193 New Year's Day:
The very beginning of
Another dreamt-away year.

194 New Year's Day—
Princess Yang-kuei-fei
Steps into the rest room.

195 Everyone can dare
To bear what's
Easy to bear;
Truly to bear is to bear
What's hard to bear.

Endurance 196
Revealed vividly:
The snow-clad bamboo.

Patience enhances 197
Your samadhi power,
Patience with others
Is for
Yourself.

Mind of the water-dipper 198
Moving between
Cold Hell and Hot Hell:
No mind,
No pain.

Mind of the water-dipper 199
Moving between
Cold Hell and Hot Hell:
With this mind,
You're free from pain.

Trees have branches, 200
Bamboos, knots;
You and I have these
Bills on file.

201 Wish I could let them
Listen to the sound
Of snow falling
At midnight in the old temple
Of Shinoda forest.

202 We know the Dharma is true
As it's
Being preached;
But we forget
As we leave the zendo.

203 Ears
Hear and eyes
See,
Then what does
Mind do?

204 Listening,
Listening
No-minded . . .
Why, it's me,
The sound of the valley!

205 Out the train window:
Scarecrows whiz by,
And people, too.

"Mad old woman," 206
You've called me, but
Soon I'll be a
Bride in the Pure Land.

Coming to the forest 207
Only to find it here as well:
The heat of the forest.

Sometimes disagreeable 208
Winds come, nevertheless
The willows—

Yesterday, today, tomorrow, 209
On the log bridge
Of this floating world,
All travelers,
Make steady steps!

The man I saw yesterday, 210
What's become of him?
Today: under the tomb.
Tomorrow someone'll ask about me,
"What's become of him?"

211 Not yesterday's,
Not tomorrow's, but
Today's cherry flowers!

212 No more, thank you, of
This suffocating world!
I'm moving to
A new house
Down in hell.

213 Besides yourself
To whom shall I show
These plum flowers?
Their color, their fragrance,
Only those in the know, know.

214 How I wish I could change
Your mind into a clear mirror
And reflect
My mind in it!

215 Unseen,
Unnoticed,
But dust will
Gather naturally
In the sleeves.

Counting the number of 216
Remaining days
One, two, three . . .
Until my fingers all stand:
The end of the year.

Today's praise, 217
Tomorrow's abuse:
It's the human way.
Weeping, laughing . . .
All utter lies.

Paulownia leaves fall 218
Rustling rustling rustling
In the autumn winds.

Duty and humanity 219
Are often incompatible:
The road forks—
But my body is one.

The man who jilted her, 220
The pebble she stumbled over,
Both prompt her to look back
With complex regret.

221 Watching, watching my step
Only to slip—
The snowed-over path.

222 The grasses and trees, too,
Seem happy this
New Year's Day morning.

223 Even mindless grasses
And trees will become
Buddhas, they say.
Then I, with mind, can attain—
How nice!

224 As if opening its mouth,
Revealing its bowels:
Pomegranate.

225 Voiceless trees and grasses
Deep in the mountains
Invite us with their
Flowers and blossoms.

Everything he says is 226
Against Buddhas and Patriarchs;
He's absorbed in love sparks,
Not seeking satori.

When asked: 227
"Where are you from?"
"Where were you born?"
Just answer: "From the
Original Nothing."

Kunisada Chūji, 228
Fearful as a devil,
Cuts and kills men—
With a sweet smile!

How funny! Bodhidharma's 229
Nine years of zazen.
What on earth did he seek?
To the satori eye,
Nothing exists from the beginning.

A cloud splits open 230
Shooting forth the moon;
One cuckoo's cry!

231 The cloud-sash,
The mist-robe,
They're worn out:
The snow-skin
Is showing.

232 Jump
Into the sky
Over those clouds,
And you'll see the moon
Even on a rainy day.

233 If cloud is sash
And rain
A robe,
Under a clear sky—
You'll all be naked!

234 Our storehouse sold off,
They enjoy sunshine now:
Peonies.

235 In the dark
I lost sight of
My shadow;
I've found it again
By the fire I lit.

Coming out of darkness 236
I'm likely to enter
The darker path again.
Shine far all over,
Moon on the mountain edge.

He's coming—coming— 237
I walked out my gate, only to
Hear pine winds from the beach
Passing by—

When you're 238
Beyond
Pain and pleasure,
Both good and bad
Fail to reach you.

So well made-up 239
They don't look like themselves:
Plum flowers on a
Snowy morning.

Smoky for a while, but 240
Soon makes it easier to sleep:
Mosquito-killing incense.

241 With heaven and earth,
Stored in his stomach,
Rice planting.

242 Heaven and earth
Stomach and all forgotten,
Rice planting.

243 When I see
Heaven and earth as
My own garden,
I live that moment
Outside the universe.

244 Feeling happy
With my children,
Finally realizing
My thoughtlessness
Toward my parents.

245 Love too
Is
Rooted in
Piss
And shit.

Falling in love with you, 246
Deep in love with you;
This secret love of mine,
Why don't you know?

Love takes her 247
Straight to the other bank
Crossing the current
Just like a ferryboat.

I surely hear its voice, but 248
Can't see it; in the garden
Just the rustling
Of pine trees.

A firefly burns itself 249
With love
Silently.
Its unspoken feeling may be
Far deeper than words.

Paradise is 250
None of my business, but
I've got to go
Help Amitabha Buddha
Who works there.

251 Where is heaven?
Very simple:
It's where you're
Lying asleep
Drunk.

252 A wish
To go to
Heaven is
The very beginning of
Falling into hell.

253 In Paradise, too,
Everything goes like this:
Full moon in summer.

254 Both heaven and hell
Are inside
Yourself;
Devils or Buddhas are
Nothing but your heart.

255 Destined to heaven
Or to hell:
Some are delighted
And others grieved,
But all are deceived.

Mind is the one 256
That reminds you
Of your illusory mind;
Always mind your mind,
Just mind! Mind!

To sleep on the pillow 257
With the moon
In perfect peace:
What a joy!

What is it 258
That you call
Your mind?
Your original mind is
"Nothing" from the beginning.

Turn your mind into 259
Rocks and trees, then
Even the busy streets
Will be nothing but paradise,
"A busy-street paradise."

How nice to understand 260
Directly from mind to mind,
Not minding the difference
Of personalities!

261 Mind?
There's nothing
Like that really.
If so, what's satori?
Who gets what?

262 What is
Mind like,
I wonder.
It's invisible, and
As large as the universe.

263 What's
Mind?
The sounds of pine winds
Drawn on the scroll
In India ink.

264 Make your mind
Flexible as water:
Now square,
Now round—up to
The shape of the bowl.

265 Your hands and feet
May belong to you, but
Can you
Always make them move
The way you want?

See how the cherry flowers 266
In the Yoshino Mountains
Let nightingales chirp
And so invite us.

Even I, 267
A no-minded monk,
Can feel
An autumn evening in
The valley where woodcocks fly.

Feeling helpless, I go out 268
To meet the moon
Only to find every mountain
Veiled with cloud.

When the east winds blow, 269
Send me your fragrance,
Plum flowers—
Though I'm not home,
Don't forget each spring.

If you get used to 270
Being satisfied, you'll be
Endlessly dissatisfied. Find
Satisfaction in dissatisfaction
And your mind will be at peace.

271 With these children
Here in this village, bouncing
A ball all day . . .
I wish the spring sun would
Never set in the west!

272 I don't know if we'll
Suffer from rain or wind
This fall, but
I'll weed my rice field,
My job for today.

273 If you grasp
The heart of this sutra,
You'll know the voices
Of merchants and customers
Preach the Dharma.

274 This road—
No one going down it but me—
Autumn evening.

275 Never regard this world as
The only one;
The next world
And the one after the next . . .
All the worlds are here now.

The monkey showman feeds 276
Fruit to his monkey;
The monkey makes its
Master make
Money by its tricks.

See those 277
Scattered pine needles:
Paired even after they wither
And fall on the ground.

If I do it like this, 278
The result will be like this:
But fully knowing that,
I'm suffering like this.

This is what 279
Keeps our life going on:
The cool of evening.

Looks threatening, 280
Menacing, but falls
Shattering to bits:
A gargoyle on the roof.

281 Why tie your horse
To the cherry tree in bloom?
When the horse becomes restless
The blossoms fall.

282 As I stumble on the slope,
My lantern has gone out;
I'm treading all alone
In complete darkness.

283 Sweat runs on my face
Upside down:
Rice planting.

284 Everyone admires
Beautiful flowers in bloom,
But the ones who know
Visit them
After they've fallen.

285 Until it blooms, we
Just think of it as a weed:
The wild chrysanthemum!

Looking down on 286
This floating world full of
Cherry flowers,
High up, elated chirping:
A skylark.

Without wine, 287
How can they become mine?
Those cherry blossoms.

The wine works now; 288
My mind grows into
Spring merriment—even
Bill-collectors' voices turn to
Nightingales' song.

Peach blossoms: 289
Now open and soon to fall, only
To open again next year.
How limitless
Their life force!

Right now, right here 290
Today—
That's your business;
Yesterday has gone forever,
Tomorrow not yet come.

291 In zazen:
Everyone coming and going
Over the bridges are
As trees
Deep in the mountains.

292 Well, is it the moon overhead
That cried?
A cuckoo.

293 Satori is something
Hung
From
The eyebrows:
Too close to see.

294 In satori,
There's neither empty sky
Nor samadhi, but
Narrow-mindedly
You regard the void as a hole.

295 Even after satori:
Willows just as
Green as before.

To the satori eye, everything 296
Melts into nothing,
Traceless—
A snowman.

Loneliness extends 297
Far and wide—up to where?
An autumn evening.

Everything 298
Changing
In this floating world.
One thing staying the same:
Death.

Mourners gathered together, 299
Each bearing his, her, its own sadness:
Recumbent image of Buddha.

If I sleep drunk 300
Protected from the cold,
Even this grass hut is
A jeweled bed.

301 A monkey has jumped—
One branch of the pine on the peak
Is green.

302 Throwing his teacher down
Is the way to show gratitude:
Sumo wrestler.

303 In hell, too, is there
The shade of a tree?
A summer afternoon.

304 The lion's roaring outburst
Blasts the great sky and
Brings back no answer,
Neither yes nor no.

305 After forty-nine illusory
Years, he excuses himself,
In Shakyamuni's words,
"Nothing's ever preachable."

Silence! 306
Piercing the rocks—
Cicadas' cry.

Looking down, you may 307
Flatter yourself because
Nothing is superior to you.
But take off your reed-hat,
See the height of the sky!

Even strong winds are 308
Weakened by
Obedient willow twigs;
They'll never
Be broken in the storm.

I never die, 309
I don't go anywhere:
I'll just stay here.
Don't ask me anything because
I speak no word.

Rise 310
Above the clouds
For a while, and you'll
See the moon
Even on rainy nights.

311 The fruit as it hangs
Becomes a sweet cake:
Persimmon.

312 Little clear streams rustle
Down through the mountain rocks
And finally let the battleship
Float on the sea.

313 Shakyamuni,
Amitabha Buddha,
Ksitigarbha Bodhisattva:
Temporary names of
One Mind.

314 Shakyamuni,
The mischievous player, came
To this world and went away,
Leaving so many
Puzzled . . .

315 Look, Sariputra,
"Emptiness is form" indeed:
Those full-blooming flowers.

Strike the empty sky 316
With Mount Sumeru
As if it were a stone
And the void will crack into—
Two, three, four . . .

White dewdrops 317
On an autumn
Maple leaf—
Just as they are—
Tiny red balls.

Dewdrops show up 318
Indiscriminately:
Any place will do.

On an unfamiliar road, 319
Don't pretend you're
Not lost.
Just ask where you are:
It's a real shortcut.

Without it you're 320
Lost and even with it
You still get lost;
What on earth
Is the true Dharma?

321 Wrinkles,
Dotted moles,
Backbone bent,
Head bald,
Hair gray.

322 Reverence is
The source of divine favors;
Without it,
Buddhas and wooden clogs are
Only pieces of wood.

323 No use
Becoming a Buddha
After you're dead.
Be enlightened
While you're alive.

324 Loved wife, hated husband:
In the end,
Under a mossy tomb,
Both skulls.

325 Eating their lunch using
Their reed-hats as a table:
Rice planting.

How cool! 326
One wheel of the moon
Among the countless worlds.

How refreshing 327
The whinny of a packhorse
Unloaded of everything!

This coolness: 328
Since before Amitabha Buddha
Entered into Nirvana.

Ivy clinging and twining 329
Even to crooked branches:
People look up and admire
The ivy-and-pine-tree.

The shaded 330
Mind-moon
Has become perfectly clear.
Not a bit of dust:
Original body-mind world.

331 A waterwheel
Will never freeze
While working hard.

332 No good, thank you.
No bad, thank you.
No "no," please.
I prefer drinking tea,
Sometimes asleep, sometimes awake.

333 Accumulating no virtue,
Committing no sin
Throughout your life?
Buddhas won't praise you,
Kings of Hell won't scold you.

334 Good and bad, or the
Reflections in the mirror:
Watch them closely
And you'll know they're
Nothing but yourself.

335 Don't step on it!
A firefly rested there
Last night.

Don't push there— 336
I've had it happen!
That point—
And I couldn't say a word.

From inside 337
It splits open naturally
That stinging fortress
Untouchable from outside:
Chestnut shell.

Even the morning glory's 338
One-day life
Has color
Of its own.

Not dyed, 339
Everything has its
Own color.
The pine is green,
Snow is white.

Shave all those 340
Illusory
Hairs on your mind,
Before minding the
Hairs on your head.

341 There! That's it!
Watch—watch your step!
Be very careful!

342 Each seems to want
A name of its own:
Spring mountains.

343 Now I vomit
The great ocean I've
Swallowed up.
Look! All the Buddhas bobbing
Up and down the waves.

344 With the radish
He was pulling,
Pointed the right direction.

345 Even for me,
The lord of the manor:
The same heat!

Forgetting everything— 346
Even planting and singing:
Rice planting.

This human world 347
Is like
A valley stream that
Never ceases, but whose
Water always changes.

The bamboo, fallen, 348
Will stand again, while
The snow that
Bends it down
Scatters and is gone.

Fragrance wraps the one 349
Who breaks off a twig:
Plum flowers.

Itself fallen, but never 350
Letting its bow and arrow go:
A scarecrow.

351 Don't boast of
Your height,
Mount Fuji!
Sometimes a spring wind will blow
Over your head.

352 Looking into the valley
From the top of the mountain:
Melons and eggplants
In full bloom.

353 The mind of a carp climbing
Up the fall is like
A strained bowstring:
If loosened,
It will fall.

354 Without woodcutters
Gathering firewood,
How could
The chimneys in the capital
Smoke?

355 The wind brings me
Enough fallen leaves
To make a fire.

Bamboo and sparrow, good friends; 356
But once bamboo becomes
A catching rod,
They're enemies.

A bamboo shoot grows 357
Crooked, stretching
Out of the hedge.

Climbing 358
Deep into the mountains
Only to see
The moon in the cloud,
The dew on the leaves.

Several standing 359
Pine trees
Tied into
Natural pillars:
A logger's hut.

The mind of the person 360
In front of you is
A mirror;
Watch the reflection of
Your mind in it.

361 Shoot an arrow
With a stringless bow
Against no target!
It never hits, but
It never misses.

362 Standing like a peony,
Sitting, a lotus,
And she's like a lily
Walking.

363 Whatever happens to me
Concerns me not at all.
I could throw my life away
For your sake!

364 Let's enjoy
Today
Calmly;
Yesterday's gone,
Tomorrow's unknown.

365 My joy is:
Sake before me,
Pillar behind to lean on,
My best friend,
Sound of *miso* grinding.

My joy: 366
Cherry blossoms in spring,
Moon in autumn,
Three meals every day
In family harmony.

I ask you, 367
Please blow against me
And wake me up
If I should fall into a doze:
Pine wind from the mountaintop.

How nice it is! 368
No speck of dust
That doesn't contain
All the Buddhas
From every direction.

Deceive me, if you will, 369
I'll let you do that.
But, I—I'll never
Never deceive you.

Meeting at night 370
After long separation . . .
How hateful! The sounds
Of the morning bell.

371 Hey, Bodhidharma, let's go
Cherry-flower-viewing tomorrow,
Shave your whiskers.

372 Dandelions, how many days
Have we been stepping on you?
Today, you bloom.

373 Dandelions,
Though we step on you,
You never stop smiling.

374 Your parents,
Grandparents . . .
All constituted in Yourself.
Love Yourself,
Revere Yourself.

375 Butterflies:
They do not quarrel over
Flowers up or down.

In shallow water, you tuck 376
Your clothes up; but as it
Grows deeper, you'll be tucking
Naked.

The world of "dust" is 377
An absolute lie; see
The snow this morning!

Cherry blossoms are 378
Very much admired because
They fall;
But yet,
Yet . . .

Flowers fall, 379
Returning to
Dust . . .
Why do you stick to them,
Butterfly?

I know this is the 380
Final road each of us must
Go along; but I didn't expect
Yesterday was that day for him,
Today for her.

381 Be careful
Every minute, reminding yourself:
One moment's
Carelessness may cause
A thousand-mile difference.

382 The moon is set;
My shadow has become
Myself.

383 The moon is sinking,
Our conversation never ending . . .
Oh, please stop
The dawn bell ringing.

384 The moon on each rice field
Is only a reflection;
The true moon lives
There in the sky.

385 The moon is me?
Or me, the moon?
The indivisible
Me-and-moon
In the early morning sky.

Moonlight— 386
The Four Gates and Four Schools
Are nothing but one.

See through 387
Yourself before
You were born;
Complete Nothingness,
Even no parents to love.

Don't step 388
Out of the usual way:
Hazy moon.

If anyone 389
Sins, please blame me,
O Heaven, because
All people are
My own children.

Hatred like layers of snow 390
Melts into
A spring river as if
Breaking into a smile.

391 The moon is shining
On each dewdrop
On each grass blade.

392 This dewlike world,
Indeed fleeting like dew;
Yet, yet . . .

393 Don't pick it up,
Just leave it there:
A clover in the field.

394 The moon in
The water in my palms,
The moon on
The wide river:
No difference.

395 While everyone
Washes his dirty
Hands and feet,
Few remove
Stains from their minds.

392

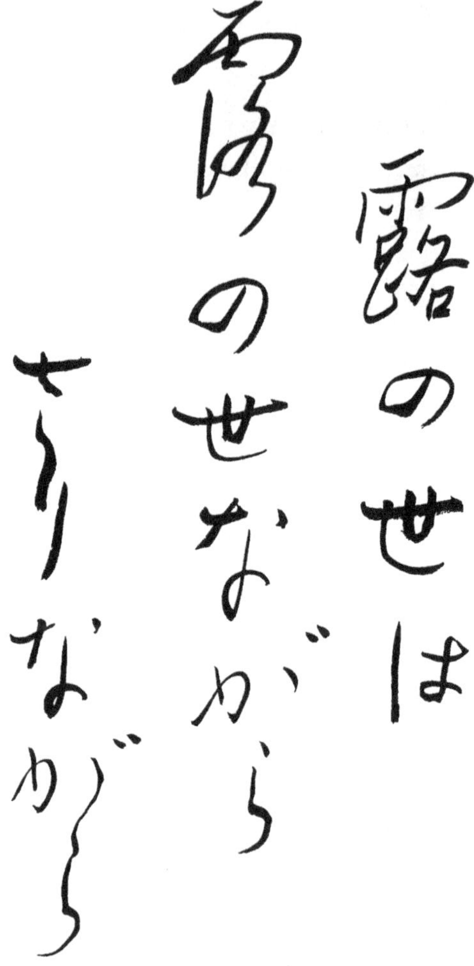

396 Two-hands clapping . . .
The maid serves tea;
Birds fly up;
Fish come closer
In Sarusawa Pond.

397 A hand-rolled
Dumpling of
Heaven-and-earth:
I've gulped it down
And easily it went.

398 I've thrust away
The man who gulped the dumpling
Of heaven-and-earth
With the
Tip of my eyelash.

399 Having now stored
Heaven and earth in his stomach:
Beggar.

400 Both the noble
And the humble
Become smoke
Of one color
Over Toribe Hill.

It couldn't care less 401
Whose soil it may become:
Falling leaf.

In my old age, I 402
Look back on the bridge of
This floating world.
Goodness! How could I have
Passed such a dangerous one!

An old man has 403
A hard time:
People treat him
Lightly, yet
Heavily he has to move.

In chanting-samadhi, 404
No myself,
No Buddha: only
Voices resounding . . .
"Namu Amida-butsu!"

In chanting-samadhi, 405
No myself,
No Buddha:
"Namu Amida-butsu!"
"Namu Amida-butsu!"

406 Rising to the surface with
The strength it jumped with:
A frog.

407 See that stupid frog?
Hopped too high,
Missed its food.

408 When the lantern goes out,
Where, I wonder, does
Its light go?
Darkness is my own
Original house.

409 Even the guardian deity
With tiger's courage
Turns into a mouse
When he meets mercy.

410 A tiger leaps
A thousand-mile forest; but
To me it's not easy to open
Your creaking door.

I've caught you, 411
Amitabha Buddha, I
Won't let you go.
Hey, come along with me
Down to hell.

You call me 412
Good-for-nothing. Yes, but
Good-for-nothing is sometimes
Good for everything!

The man forsaken 413
On Toribe Hill,
What has become of him?
The answer is: the white
Dew on the grave.

The one who robs 414
And the one who is robbed
Are alike:
The cloud going
And coming in the sky.

Though you live in the mud, 415
Your heart is pure and your
Beautiful flowers regale our eyes:
Lotus plant.

416 I've caught a robber
Only to find he is
My own son:
Hang him—
Release him—

417 Even muddy water
Becomes dew: pearly beads
On the lotus leaf.

418 Off dragonfly-catching,
How far, I wonder,
Have they been, today?

419 What is this seed, a mustard
Or a poppy? It's hard to tell
Which is which.
But when fully grown,
The flowers will tell.

420 Even in the dew
On the tiny blade
Of some nameless grass,
The moon
Will show itself.

Change your name, 421
Pretty rape flowers on
Sacred Kōya Mountain.

If you want 422
To live long,
Just work.
Look, running water
Never stagnates.

We wish 423
Our lives were long
While our hair's
Growing long
Is a nuisance.

A long day— 424
Yet want more time to sing,
Larks in the sky.

The mouth 425
Of a priest who
Makes long sermons:
I feel like punching
A thousand . . . two thousand . . .

426 Sometimes a cloud will
Half hide the moon,
But it's
The moon's accessory,
Enhancing its beauty.

427 It's comfortable to live
Deep in the mountains because
Grasses and trees
Never say
Yes and no.

428 Warriors, farmers,
Artisans, and tradesmen—
I wish all, on good terms,
Would cross this floating world
On the same ferryboat!

429 There, it's flowing,
One red maple leaf,
Bobbing in the stream.

430 Even the valley water,
Bound to become ocean,
Goes
For some time
Under the leaves of trees.

Which shows the truth, 431
Crying or not crying?
A cicada and a firefly are
Fighting for the truth.

The word "nothing" 432
Soon reminds us
Of "everything"
Without knowing that
It's it just as it is.

"There's nothing," 433
And we think
There's nothing at all;
But listen, that echo
Really answers.

Nothing is there 434
But reflected there:
A moon in the water.

Our lives are as 435
Fleeting as dew . . .
Everyone knows this, so
Why do we wet our sleeves
Whenever one of us disappears?

436 In summer
Everywhere is
Summer;
In winter, everywhere is
Winter.

437 I have spent
Many summer nights
Fully awake:
I have so many things
To worry about for the world.

438 Summer grasses:
Remains of the dreams
Of soldiers long ago.

439 Let your mind be
Vacant like the cast-off shell
Of a summer cicada
And then you'll have
Nothing to be afraid of.

440 Not by a harsh slap,
But by a tender pat,
More tears fall.

What are you worrying about, 441
Riverside willow?
You pass every day
  Just gazing at the stream.

  I don't know 442
What's there inside,
  But I feel, somehow,
Tears flowing
Out of reverence.

  I don't know why, 443
But I feel sad
  When I see
A dawn moon over the hill
With a monkey's cry echoing.

  Nothing 444
Seems to happen:
  Insects chirping.

  A person who 445
Does everything as it
  Naturally goes
Gets along easily in
This world and the next.

446 Really nothing to say
In words:
Asking itself,
Answering itself,
The sounds of pine wind.

447 Everything
Changes in this world
But flowers will open
Each spring
Just as usual.

448 Everything goes
Just as you walk:
Stepping with your
Right foot,
Then, left.

449 Remember:
Too much
Pleasure today is
Tomorrow's
Pain.

450 It depends.
In summer
The hemp robe
Is better than
The brocade.

Everything is
A lie in this world
Because even
Death
Isn't so. 451

The yellow-flower field:
The moon is in the east,
The sun in the west. 452

Hating the sound of the waves,
Living in the mountains now
Only to find the wind in
The pine trees noisier. 453

Almighty Amitabha Buddha:
I thought it was
Buddha's name,
But it's the very person
Who is chanting here now. 454

Even on the peony flowers
Of the old capital Nara
Scattering dung:
Herds of deer . . . 455

456 Only for fun I planted
This chrysanthemum;
What white flowers!

457 A million dollars,
Damn it! It's only a
Dewdrop on a bamboo leaf.

458 Now you have returned
Your body to
Earth-water-fire-wind;
Who is then
You?

459 You're hit, old pipe, just
To clear ashes, not because
You're hated. See, you're
Kissed—because loved!

460 Even if someone
Hates you,
Don't hate back:
An-eye-for-an-eye
It never ends . . .

The moon reflects 461
Even on dirty water;
This realized,
Our mind
Clears up.

When the water 462
In your mind
Clears up,
Calm stars can be seen
Reflected on it.

Westward— 463
Eastward—
Wherever it is,
Grasses follow the direction
Of whatever wind blows.

Far, far to the west, beyond 464
A million billion Buddha-lands,
Amitabha Buddha lives. But,
Open your eyes wide and he's
Here before you.

In the daytime, 465
My silhouette
Lies by my feet.

466 Komachi, fairest girl in Japan,
Sixteen years old now:
Her sweet dimple
Will shatter castles.

467 The surface of the garden
Is not yet dry after
The evening shower.
But look! That clear
Moon in the sky.

468 If you're a plum,
I'll be a willow;
Our matchmaker
The blowing spring wind.

469 If I'm with you—going
Into a desert
With only a pan and saucers—
I wouldn't care a bit!

470 I can surmount
All difficulties,
Overcome any hardship
If I'm by your side.

The best 471
Defense
Against a thief is
Not a six-foot rod,
But poverty.

The burglar has 472
Forgotten to steal:
The moon in the window.

The robber, too, is 473
Robbed of his
Original treasure:
The straightforward
Mind.

See those rats biting 474
The boards of the cupboard;
Those sons who bite
Their parents' purse.

Asleep or awake, 475
Awake or asleep,
I think of you,
Of you—only of you.

476 It's your lips
That invite
Friendship;
And your lips that
Send your friends away.

477 Too much
Sutra chanting is
Useless:
You might even
Pass through paradise.

478 Sutra chanting
With your mind
Somewhere else:
It accumulates no virtue
Like talking in sleep.

479 Wholehearted
Sutra chanting is
Your master.
Keep out that
Familiar guest: illusion.

480 I'm a wind bell
Hung from the eaves;
Whether I ring or not,
Depends on the wind.

480

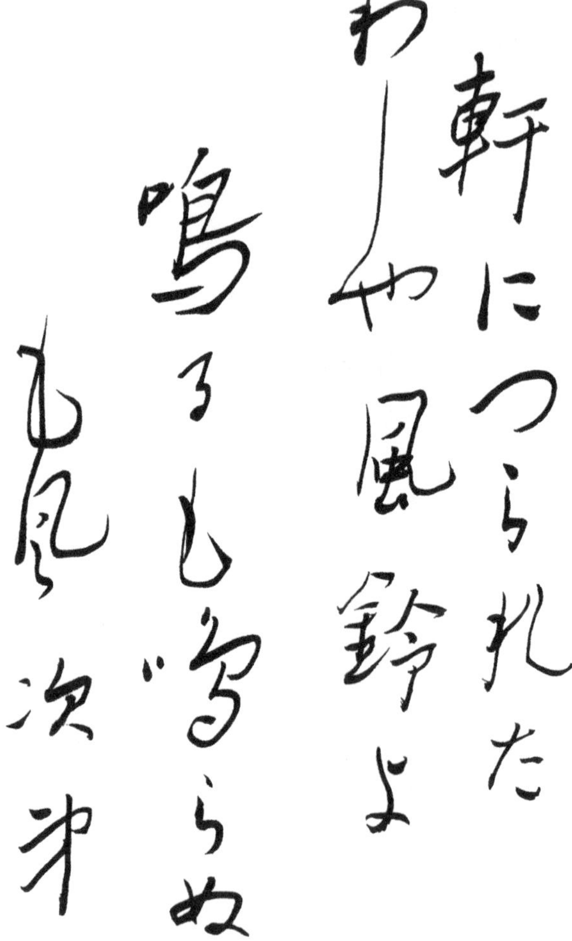

481 How nice! All scattered,
Nothing left at all:
Cherry trees.

482 I know well enough these
Cherry blossoms will
Return to dust, but I
Find it hard to leave
The trees in full bloom.

483 What peace it is
Going to the shrine with
Nothing to pray for!

484 Had better not kill
Lice and mosquitoes;
Squash your self.

485 The sea of Dharma:
However deep
It may be—
I'll dip and dip it up
Until it's dry.

If you drink wine, 486
You'll naturally get drunk;
Lotus flowers may fall, but will
Surely come out again.

Carefree fools 487
Free from seeds of contention:
Easy for them
To be broad-minded.

Around the graveyard's 488
Mossy tombs,
Insects chirping, chirping—
But no sutra chanting.

Better making money in trade 489
Cheerfully clapping
These two hands
Than listening to Hakuin's
One-handed clapping.

Dust collects 490
Soon after it's cleaned out:
Endless repetition . . .
Likewise, the human mind,
The garden with falling leaves.

491 Beyond those new cherry leaves—
Echoes of voices
Of those who know.

492 For shame!
The bottle splashes noisily
Because it's not full.

493 Spread of the banana leaf:
One day's journey
For the snail.

494 A lotus flower is white,
Though around it
The water is muddy.

495 The flag flaps,
Your mind flaps; then,
Unfurl your mind,
Show its flapping!

Farming: 496
People come home, bowing
To the evening sun.

In my bowl there's enough 497
Rice for tomorrow; how cool
This summer evening!

He-and-she news 498
Spreads fast;
Their story began in the rain
Under an umbrella.

Plausible lies, 499
Eight hundred are
Never
Superior to
Honesty.

Flowers in full bloom, 500
At their best
For only three days.

501 A wild rose
Sometimes flowers,
Sometimes turns into needles:
But does it have
Any double intention?

502 Flowers
Will open
Again next spring
But my dead child will
Never come again.

503 Transient as a flower,
But not so pretty:
The human mind.

504 March, the flower time: even
Little birds dance, calling
"Hey, butterflies!
Hey, flowers!"

505 In full-blooming March
Each with a bottle,
Each with a Kasyapa smile,
Cherry-flower-viewing wine.

I want to ask the butterfly 506
About the flowers' dreams, alas—
It has no voice!

In bloom for a while, 507
Then turns into a
Bitter sheath:
A pepper.

Perennial flowers 508
Return to their roots, and birds
To their old nests;
But, no man can return
To his younger days.

After flowers and red leaves 509
Are gone,
We know the chastity
Of the pine tree.

Viewing cherry flowers, 510
Drinking wine,
Bodhidharma with whiskers will
Show up from somewhere.

511 For those who wait only
For flowers to bloom,
I wish I could show them
The spring grass in
The snow of a mountain village.

512 Like the flowers you watch,
Your steps are directed
Toward the end of life.

513 Don't move
Or you're done for!
See that five-inch nail
Driven in the straw doll.

514 Women on the coast, too,
Wear grass coats in the rain
Till they reach the sea.

515 Originally there's
No dust to sweep off:
The mind of the person
Who holds the broom is
Exactly like the dirt.

This is the broom for 516
Sweeping away:
The man who
Insists that he has
No dust to clear.

Anger makes 517
A person forget
This world, the next worlds,
Other people,
And himself.

In the evening when 518
Leaves fall by
Ones and twos,
You can hear the sounds
Of not-falling rain.

The beam that 519
Rats run along
May be one pathway,
But human beings must walk
The true Way.

When spring comes, 520
My thatched-roof hut
Is very nice;
On the eave's edge,
Nightingales come and sing.

521 When spring comes,
Prepare clothes
For summer.
Don't waste
Even a day.

522 Spring has come:
All over the capital
And countryside,
Pines are green
And flowers are red.

523 Spring is gone:
On the twigs
Behind the green leaves,
Young plum fruit,
Two, three, four . . .

524 In spring, flowers
Giving off fragrance;
Seeing their faces,
I feel like
Smiling back.

525 The spring sea:
Slowly swelling and rolling
All day long.

Spring grass: 526
Burnt, but soon growing
Green, green . . .

The whole spring field is 527
Swallowed at a gulp:
A pheasant's cry.

In spring, flowers; 528
Summer, cuckoos;
Autumn, moon.
In winter, snow is
Chilling and cool.

Spring rain 529
Falls everywhere
Without discrimination,
But each grass and tree shows
Different colors.

Spring rain: good for 530
Planting chrysanthemums,
Good for napping, too.

528

春は花夏ほとゝ
ぎす秋は月
冬雪さえて冷し
かりけり

Mount Fuji— 531
On a fine day, it's good.
Cloudy, also very good.
Its original form
Never changes.

Scatter ten thousand 532
Troubles with a single smile:
Plum flowers.

No carpenter 533
Will build a
Wagon-on-fire;
We make it for ourselves
And ride on it.

The sun is my eye; 534
The open sky is my form;
Wind, my breath;
Seas and mountains,
My whole body.

Pull and bind the sheaves 535
Of grass together:
There's a grass hut.
Untie them and, there,
The original field.

536 Pull and bind the sheaves
Of grass together:
There's a grass hut.
Without untying them, there,
The original field.

537 Though no one lives now
In this mountain village,
When spring comes,
Willows are green,
Flowers red.

538 Someone else's question,
Somehow
You can answer;
But, your mind's question,
How can you answer?

539 Serving for others,
Itself becomes naked:
A cotton bush.

540 A person who
Speaks ill of others
To your face
Surely speaks ill of you
Behind your back.

Learn from others; 541
Yourself well disciplined,
Get on with your
   Bodhisattva Way.

   In the winter field, 542
No man but
   Dry bamboo leaves; see,
The empty sky talks,
The stone woman smiles back.

   The taste of cold water 543
Drunk up in a gulp
   In summer heat:
Hard to speak of in words,
Never explained.

   I wish our minds 544
Were equal to the color
   Of pine trees
And wish our promise
Would keep its green forever.

   A rain shower, then 545
Back to the original
   Moonlit night.

546 Coming alone?
Going alone?
It's an illusion.
I'll show you the way of
No-coming-and-no-going.

547 Arriving alone,
Returning alone,
This lonely way:
It's strange for a preacher
To preach the way.

548 Day after day,
Day by day,
Dust of mind collects;
Be sure to wash it away
And find your original Self.

549 Though separated by
A hundred miles, two hundred miles,
We see the same
Moon in the cloud.

550 When your robe of
Fallen leaves
Wears out, it's
Best to wait in your hut
For a winter storm.

Samadhi is like 551
This empty sky;
Instead of entering it,
Narrow-mindedly
You fall into a pit.

Floating clouds— 552
When wind blows, they'll follow;
No wind and they don't move.
Everything's up to the wind,
Life without worry.

White snow on Mount Fuji 553
Melts in the rising sun;
Rice cakes this morning
Melt in the boiling pot.

The two plum trees: 554
One opens early, the other late.
I love them both.

Dharma is 555
A doorknob,
A pine on the hill,
A flint bag,
And a nightingale's chirp.

556 The pen is truly mighty:
Over seas and mountains,
Sending news back and forth
Connecting you and me.

557 The jewel
Is in your bosom;
Why look for it
Somewhere
Else?

558 The ship depends on sail,
The sail depends on wind;
I, a merchant,
Depend on the customers.

559 Calling for a boat—
Only the river mist
Answers me.

560 Though you're trod upon,
Endure it, be patient,
Roadside weed!
Spring comes soon
And your flowers will open.

Reading books: 561
The writers are no more
People of long ago,
But your friends
Now, here, before you.

Some in bloom, some scattering, 562
They're too beautiful
To step on, but otherwise
No one can walk on the path:
Mountain cherry flowers.

One in evening dress, 563
The other in house frock:
There's a big difference.
But, when they're naked,
Almost the same.

Layers of snow 564
Melting
In the morning sun;
The faint sounds of dripping
Heard from the roof.

I don't know 565
The mind
Of the old pond;
But I can still hear
The frog's splash.

566 The old pond:
A frog hops in,
The sound of the water.

567 Since I don't have
My
Native town,
Wherever I may go,
I'm on my way home.

568 Push aside
Those leaves heaped on
The old path;
You'll see the invisible footprints
Of the Sun Goddess.

569 Pine trees in the wind
Don't break;
They always scatter
The snow before it's
Too heavy for their branches.

570 Farts, too, are
Sacred. See, even
Their sounds
Suggest Buddha:
"Booooooo."

Concentrate your mind 571
Inside your navel,
Penetrate the truth:
Life and death are
An out-and-out lie.

Ungrateful cucumber 572
Grows big,
Breaking the fence
That helped it.

Mosquito larvae, 573
Swimming up and down
Until they grow up.

The Lotus Sutra 574
Isn't limited to
Eight volumes;
Pine, bamboo, cherry, each
Demonstrates its meaning.

Desire, regret, 575
Hatred, affection,
Once rid of them all,
This world is
Yours.

576 As many people as
The stars in the sky . . .
But, the moon is
Only you.

577 If you want to
Know Buddha, it's pointless
To seek him in the temple;
The Buddha is simply you
Wishing to see Buddha.

578 The mind seeking Buddha
Outside
Is
The worst
Illusion of all.

579 Charity appears
To reduce what's yours
For a while, but
In the end you're
Enriched.

580 A cuckoo's cry:
The mountain must be
In that direction,
So, steer the boat this way,
Boatman in the dark night.

I glance toward 581
The direction where
A cuckoo cried
Only to find the dawn moon
Still in the sky.

The well of no width, no depth: 582
There, brimming water ripples
Without wind. See that
Formless person
Dipping up the water.

On my way to you 583
A thousand miles become one;
Across the wide rice field,
Just a jump—

On my way to you, 584
A thousand miles become one:
Having missed you . . .
A thousand on the way back.

Slipping in the tub 585
When you're in love:
Even muddy water tastes as
Sweet as dew.

583

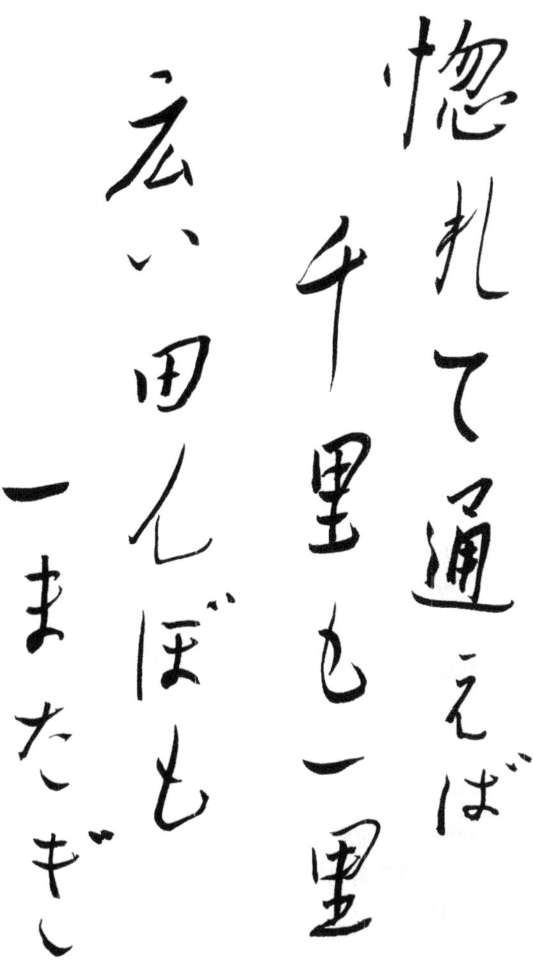

Whoop—whoop— 586
Mountain birds
Whoop—
I wonder if they are the
Father and mother I loved.

Our illusions are 587
The beginning of
Satori;
See how sour grapes
Become sweet raisins.

I am 588
Originally "Nothing"
And timeless;
Nowhere to go
Even after death.

As the path winds, 589
Growing on either side,
Fluttering in the wind:
Pampas grass.

Wrong if you regard 590
Underdogs
As always weak:
Sometimes they're very wise
And know what's what.

591 Sown seeds
Bring forth buds;
Planted seedlings grow.
Oh, the limitless blessing
Of heaven and earth.

592 Mutual trust shrinks
A thousand miles to one:
You're safe
And I'm sound.

593 Pine winds,
Moonlight on the field grasses
Are all that I have:
Besides,
No visitors.

594 Waiting, waiting
For news of you;
How are you
Getting on, I wonder?

595 Playing with the firefly
Caught by my beckoning fan—
Sort of killing time while
I wait for you.

My hat worn slantwise— 596
Everything up to heaven—
In travel a companion,
In life compassion.

With no intention 597
To defend
The hillside rice field,
It provides no small service:
The scarecrow.

If illusion is a dream, 598
Satori is also a dream:
Awakening from a dream
Is the beginning of life.

When you feel 599
You're living in illusion,
You are in satori;
If you're sure of satori,
You're living in illusion.

Illusory mind is 600
The beginning of satori:
The moon dwells even
In dirty water.

601 Your illusion
Divides heaven-and-hell
In two; but each is
Just a name for
The one Original Mind.

602 Don't hesitate,
Go straight on!
A snow-covered path.

603 So the full moon is admired
Like a well-rounded mind
But once it was a
Sharp-edged crescent.

604 Be round,
Thoroughly round,
Human mind!
Square minds
Often scratch.

605 You may try to be round,
But keep one corner,
O mind,
Otherwise you'll
Slip and roll away.

Although you keep 606
A jewel within yourself,
Nobody will notice it
Unless you
Polish and brighten it.

The meek-minded 607
Person who
Acts lightly
Seems unreliable, but is
Most surefooted.

A wooden pestle in a mortar 608
Grinds itself away
Gradually at each turn
Working for others' sake:
Do you know this subtle way?

Some people 609
Give themselves up
To save our world,
For shame! I stay in the
Shelter of a grass hut.

Our mind 610
And every kind of jewel:
If you polish them
They will shine
Accordingly.

611 You may brush it diligently, but
Since it's essentially iron,
Someday the rust
Will ooze out.

612 The two palms in *gasshō*:
Right, the enlightened;
Left, the unenlightened.
Between them,
One cry of Buddha.

613 That virtuous pine branch:
I'd love to see it
As an ornament
In my *tokonoma*.

614 Reflected in the water or
In the recess of a field,
Moonlight doesn't change
No matter where.

615 While faithfully throwing their
Shadows to the water,
Flirting with the wind:
Willows by the river.

I wish I could be 616
The water in the spring;
How cool it is,
The moon in summer!

More fleeting 617
Than the letters written
On water
Is our mind seeking
Buddha.

No sound is heard 618
In the creeks where
Water runs deep;
Shallow streams
Always splash.

A waterfowl, 619
Coming and going,
Leaves no trace, but
Never
Forgets its way.

A water bird 620
Lives on the water, but its
Wings aren't soaked;
Does salt permeate
Fish in the sea?

621 Even a fan, if forsaken
And neglected, will grow cross,
Blocking the way, or causing
Troubles somewhere.

622 I would head up there
To sweep off those clouds
Covering the moon,
Were there a
Road leading to it.

623 Go along the broad street!
Just go straight!
The small ones are often
Blind alleys.

624 No path runs
And no one comes
On this mountain.
What! Right here
The embers of firewood.

625 A fallen
Stone monument
By the road
Is buried in a heap
Of scattered leaves.

In spring, 626
All the grasses are
The same green;
In autumn, they show
Various colors.

The moon reflected 627
On the bottom of the pond,
There it surely is,
But how can you reach it?
Sarusawa Pond.

Our dirty water 628
Of greed, rage, and folly:
All flow into
The river that separates
This world and the next.

Colors of the mountains 629
And the murmuring of valleys
Are the forms and
Voices of
Our Shakyamuni Buddha.

As they grow up, 630
Their ears hang lower:
Rice plants.

631 Look with your ears,
Listen with your eyes,
Then you'll believe it:
A drop of water
From the eaves.

632 A horned owl,
Seeking a bare branch in
The midst of flowers.

633 They leave everything up to
The viewer's mind:
Plum and willow flowers.

634 No-minded:
I see things
Just as they are.
Why, it's me,
That star in the heavens.

635 This is this,
That is that,
Everything as it is:
A pine tree is green,
A flower is red.

How do you see 636
This morning's dew
Disappear
Before a single, ephemeral
Morning glory opens?

Looks cute, but it 637
Stings! What shall I do?
Throw it away? Or keep it?
A devil's thistle.

Eyes see many things, 638
Oars can feel the riverbed;
But why doesn't my
Longing reach you at all?

Watch the white waves 639
Rolling back to the sea
Above the clashing currents
Between the river stream
And the sea tide.

Look around, notice 640
Some well made, some clumsy:
Scarecrows.

641 I went too deep
Into the mountains and,
Looking around,
Found myself down in
Another village again.

642 Brocade of spring:
As far as the eyes can reach,
Willows and cherry blossoms
Here and there—
In and around the capital.

643 Everyone regards
The "Nothing"
As nothing:
Seeing nothing left after
Lotus leaves fall.

644 That guy going there,
Isn't he Seijurō?
That straw hat looks
Just like his.

645 The white dewdrops on
Blades of grass in
The field of Musashino are
The teardrops of insects
Chirping through the night.

Stepping on the grass 646
In the field of Musashino,
I listen for
The chirp of insects
My sleeves wet with dew.

That one really 647
Looks innocent;
Commits secret sins—
But innocently.

The grass hut I've built 648
Is broken now;
With nowhere to live,
How shall I get
Through this winter?

Depending on the wind: 649
Twining or untwining . . .
Meek-minded
Weeping willows.

We were long 650
On good terms,
But not since
I built an
Annex-storehouse.

651 The cloud in my heart
Has lifted at last:
One cool moon
  Afloat in the sky.

652   Your ears
See
  A purple robe;
Your eyes hear
One-hand clapping.

653 The plum blossoms in
The basement emit fragrance;
Secret love will
  Speak for itself.

654   The garden bamboos
Reveal
  The wind's invisible form:
Movement of shadows
In the moonlight.

655 The invisible wind in the sky,
In the long process of time,
Turns into flowers
  And autumn maple leaves.

Bright moon: 656
I wandered around the pond
All through the night . . .

Shining moon: 657
Shadows of the pine
Thrown on the *tatami* mat.

Full moon— 658
Everything wet with dew
Except the dew itself.

If a messenger 659
Comes from Hades
To fetch me,
Please say to him,
"He's not home now."

The other world 660
Isn't another country;
It's no other than
Satori
Three inches within your heart.

661 "Blind!" they call me,
But it's often
Those with eyes
Who are really blind.

662 Days and months go by
Rolling—rolling—
Rolling—
A waterwheel.

663 Bread and soup,
And cotton clothes
Help you,
But the other possessions
May lead you astray.

664 Eyes wide open! No easy love!
Were his skin
Peeled off, everyone's a
Shit-making machine.

665 Happy, happy
Young Pine Tree,
Branches flourishing—
Leaves also flourishing—

Your eyes, nose, and limbs 666
All may work well, but be careful!
Heaven or hell depends
Wholly on your mind.

Spring, after nine years 667
Facing the wall in zazen:
A big yawn—

The original body returns 668
Of itself to its
Original residence:
No use searching out Buddha,
It's not your business.

A slip of the tongue 669
Chills my lips;
Autumn wind—

Different places 670
Have
Different names:
Ashi in Naniwa is called
Hamaogi in Ise.

671 How light my sleeves are,
Nothing's inside:
Joy of the evening cool.

672 How sad to see
Red maple leaves falling—
Sadder to admit
Our own autumn
When we, too, will fall.

673 A yellow Japanese rose
Opens its eightfold petals,
What a pity! Those flowers
Bear no fruit.

674 Unlikely to
Die soon:
Chirrups of cicadas.

675 Burnt, and it'll
Become ash;
Buried, soil;
Then, what is it that
Remains to commit evil?

Merciful eyes 676
Make mind and manner
Meek and mild—
And words, too.

I, an innkeeper, 677
Welcome all visitors:
Shakyamuni, Confucius,
Princesses, everyone.

Give a damn! 678
Once I've been beaten,
I'll drink poison,
Eat the saucer.

Sliding shut 679
The torn paper door, I gaze
At the moon and plum flowers
Through the holes.

Whether deep in the mountains 680
Or far in the countryside,
Where you live, the same flowers
Of the capital will open.

681 No bird leaves its
Nest on the burning mountain;
Nothing in the world is
Sweeter than a child.

682 Deep in the mountains,
No one knocks on
My brushwood door
But the stormy winds
Blowing in the night.

683 It's drizzling on the
Pile of
Dry
Autumn maple leaves
Deep in the mountains.

684 The mountain man's
Wood box is raw
And unlacquered:
Nowhere is it
Faded or discolored.

685 My wish to stay
In the mountains
Aloof from the world is
A warning that I must deepen
Still my satori.

Mountain life: 686
How calm
And comfortable!
No one comes here,
I visit no one.

The evening bells 687
From the mountain temple
Sound pleasant to
The one who has secured
A lodging for the night.

The monk ringing bells 688
In the mountain temple
Doesn't show himself,
But the people nearby can
Tell what time it is.

The moon is declining on 689
The edge
Of the mountain;
How I regret the days
I have spent in vain!

He's taking a nap 690
While mountain water
Hulls the rice for him.

691 Hearing a crow with no mouth
Cry in the deep
Darkness of the night,
I feel a longing for
My father before he was born.

692 Hey, don't hit him!
The fly rubs his hands,
Rubs his legs.

693 In a dignified manner
Gazing at the mountain,
A frog.

694 The mountain winds, sweeping
Off the evening shower clouds,
Bring
Coolness for a while—
The cicadas' song.

695 Where did you sleep last night?
Tonight—here, and tomorrow
Somewhere, with the levee
In a rice field as my pillow.

The ghost has at last been
Unmasked!
Withered pampas grass. 696

A bit of rouge on the snow: 697
To the morning sun
Smiling back—
One red plum flower.

Only after severe cold 698
And snowfall, everything meets spring.
Now your time has come, plum,
Open all your blossoms!

After removing all her 699
Makeup of snow, she's really
Proud of her original face:
Mount Fuji.

Her snow-white skin 700
Wrapped in sash of mist
Attracts everyone:
Mount Fuji.

701 Even in the snow
Doesn't feel cold:
A snowman.

702 One-night lodging
For flowing water—
Thin ice.

703 Coming or going—
I'm quite free
Just like a boat drifting
As the waves move.

704 Awakened from a dream,
How ashamed!
Bed-wetting . . .

705 It's only an illusion,
Nothing much, I know; but to
Me, unenlightened one,
"Come on, honey!"

It looks as if we're 706
Talking about a dream, half asleep,
On a night of dreams
During the intervals of
Dozing . . .

Born into 707
A dream in this
World of dream, we
Vanish like a dewdrop:
What peace!

From old times, 708
Too intimate
Friendship
Ends with
Parting.

Do hermits also 709
Enjoy this scenery?
An autumn evening.

The man 710
Who's escaped the world
To live in the mountains,
If he's still weary,
Where should he go?

711 While enjoying
Mountain life
Aloof from the world,
Everyone forgets
Days and months.

712 Looking closely, I've
Found a *nazuna* blooming
Beneath the hedge.

713 So easy to judge
Your neighbor's
Faults and virtues, but
Your own—
Invisible: complete darkness.

714 I fear nothing
In this world
But a leaking roof,
A fool,
And debt.

715 Money and woman:
Those villains who often
Lead men astray.
Oh, if by some means,
I could meet them!

But for the other 716
Sex in this world,
How peaceful
The minds
Of both women and men!

Nothing in this world 717
Is more comfortable
Than sleep:
It's only fools that
Wake up and work.

Men and cigarettes 718
Are known
Only after
They've turned to
Smoke . . .

Our mind is like 719
A puppet show:
When a devil
Pushes itself forward,
A Buddha will hide.

Were 720
Everyone
Buddhas,
Shakyamuni and Bodhidharma
Would find nothing to do.

721 The whole world is
Entirely filled with the scent:
Plum blossoms.

722 Human relations are like
Those between riders
And bearers of palanquins:
For some, aching buttocks;
For others, aching shoulders.

723 Human life:
Eat and earn,
Sleep and wake.
What's next to do?
Simply to die.

724 There's no company
On this
Birth-and-death road;
It's a lonely way,
Alone coming, alone going.

725 Our world is
Like a row of
Worn stakes:
This one, too long;
That one, too short.

The only thing 726
Changeless is that everything
Changes, so
Your present grief
Will also change.

What is 727
Changeless in this world?
Tomorrow's river:
Yesterday's creek,
Today's shallows.

What shall I compare 728
This world to?
The moon reflected in the
Scattered dewdrops on the
Shaking wings of a waterfowl.

Everyone is 729
Attached to
A single surface of skin;
Peel it off and see
The beautiful and the ugly.

The fleeting world: 730
Like cherry blossoms
Unnoticed for three days.

731 Understand that
Everything in this world is
Me:
You're me,
I'm you.

732 In this world
Nothing is permanent:
See through it!
Yesterday's fire—
Today's flood—

733 The maiden flower grows
Into a full-blooming
Bride,
A fading wife,
A wrinkled old woman.

734 To what can we
Compare this world?
The white wake
Trailing behind the ship that
Set sail early in the morning.

735 To what can we compare
This world?
The traceless wake
Of the ship that set sail
Early in the morning.

Shame 736
On you,
Shameless men!
Those who feel ashamed
Often need not.

All through the night 737
I heard the sounds
Of rain, but they were the
Rustle of the leaves falling
On the old temple garden.

Throughout the night 738
I searched my
Mind:
Traces of the birds that
Flew in the sky yesterday.

All night long 739
I've chanted
All the Buddhas' names,
All of which were once
My original name.

I resolve to do it 740
Next year, next year . . . and
Each year ends.

741 A falling flower
Returning to its branch?
Butterfly.

742 Someone asks me,
"Ryōkan, what do you want
To leave after death?"
My last message is simply
"Namu-Amida-butsu!"

743 After wandering around
So many places, I've at last
Found one night's lodging.
And even that's
Not my own.

744 Ruby, diamond,
Sapphire, emerald:
What good are they
On the way to
The other world?

745 What a pity!
A person lost at
The crossroads of karma
Though right in the midst of
Paradise.

My hut's roof is 746
The blue heavens;
Floor, the earth;
Lamps, the sun and moon;
Hand-broom, the wind.

If only 747
I could tell you
How I long for you!
And how
You feel to me!

Unaware they fly away— 748
Wild geese,
Their shadows
Reflected:
The workings of the water.

Should my mind be 749
Reflected in
The mirror,
How ugly
It would be!

My mind 750
Just as it is, is
A Buddha;
Are there waves
Apart from water?

751 What shall I compare
My mind to?
Asuka River,
Your clear stream is
The moon of autumn night.

752 Even though it's only myself,
It's scary
Reflected in the water.

753 It's also mine—
Then it's not heavy:
The snow on my hat.

754 My original house:
No pillar,
No thatched roof,
Never soaked by rain,
Never blown by wind.

755 Young people,
If you care for your life,
Kill your self!
Once done,
You're deathless.

Young men these days are 756
Weak: he says, tottering,
Staggering, an old man of
  Those-were-the-days.

  A farewell: 757
Why does everyone
  Grieve?
There's no parting
From the very beginning.

Though apart from each other 758
There's not the slightest gap
Between us,
  Your-mind-my-mind.

  Divided and divided 759
And subdivided again,
  The water runs;
Do you know all streams come
From a single source?

  There are many different 760
Paths running up
  To the mountaintop,
But everyone sees
The same moon on the peak.

761 I wish I could be a
Monster,
Gulp you whole
Become one with you.

762 A woman's tongue,
Three inches long,
Rules over men,
Six feet tall.

763 Don't forget!
Harrow and seed
In spring;
Weeding in summer;
Harvest in autumn.

764 While you try
Not to forget, you're
Liable to forget;
But, after you've forgotten,
You have nothing to forget.

765 Apart from
Your self,
Watching the mind,
You'll find it's
The brightest mirror in the world.

I regard my 766
Mind as a willow:
Free and flexible,
Accepting everything.

I'm fifteen, 767
A bud of a flower;
Whose love will
Open it?

A life of poverty: 768
Keeping my mind serene,
Spending each day
In my grass hut
Just as it passes.

When I die, 769
Don't burn the corpse,
Don't bury it;
Just throw it in a field,
Feed a hungry dog!

Give up 770
Your little self,
Watch the whole universe.
See, there's
Nothing binds you.

771 Come on, let's
Play together,
Motherless sparrow!

772 No me,
No others at all, only
The huge void sky:
Oneness,
Just oneness.

773 You and I,
At each breath
Draw nearer on
The way to hell, or
To Amitabha's Pure Land.

Index of First Lines

Design by David Bullen
Typeset in Mergenthaler Bembo
by Wilsted & Taylor
Printed by Braun-Brumfield
on acid-free paper

Printed in the USA
CPSIA information can be obtained
at www.ICGtesting.com
LVHW091133150724
785511LV00001B/119

9 780865 473287